SCRATCHING MADE EASY

TURNTABLE METHOD

BY JASON E. BULLOCK & M. DWAYNE BULLOCK

Scratching Made Easy Turntable Method
Book 1: A Guide to Scratching
First Edition

By Jason E. Bullock and M. Dwayne Bullock

Illustrations by G.J. Stein
Cover Design by James T. Eagan of Bookfly Design
Editing by Ronny S. Schiff
Book Design by Charylu Roberts, O.Ruby Productions

Library of Congress Control Number: 2020925623

Library of Congress Publisher's Cataloging-in-Publication Data

Names: Bullock, Jason E., author. | Bullock, M. Dwayne, author. | Stein, G. J., illustrator.
Title: Scratching made easy turntable method. Book one, A guide to scratching / by Jason E. Bullock &
    M. Dwayne Bullock ; [illustrations by G.J. Stein].
Other Titles: Guide to scratching
Description: First edition. | Baltimore, Maryland : Scratching Made Easy, [2022]
Identifiers: ISBN 9781736221501 (paperback) | ISBN 9781736221518 (ebook)
Subjects: LCSH: Turntablism--Instruction and study. | Turntablism--
    Methods. | Phonograph turntable music. BISAC: MUSIC / Instruction &
    Study / Exercises. | MUSIC / Genres & Styles / Rap & Hip Hop. | MUSIC /
    Genres & Styles / Dance. | MUSIC / Instruction & Study / Theory.
Classification: LCC MT703 .B65 2022 (print) | LCC MT703 (ebook) | DDC 786.7--dc23

No part of this publication may be reproduced, stored in a retrieval system, or transmitted in any form or by any means, electronic, digital, mechanical, photocopying, recording, or otherwise, without written permission of the publisher.

Permissions may be sought directly via the Scratching Made Easy website.

www.scratchingmadeeasy.com

Scratching Made Easy
Apollon Music Group, LLC
Baltimore, Maryland

Copyright © 2021 Jason E. Bullock and M. Dwayne Bullock
All Rights Reserved • International Copyright Secured

To our parents —

*Without them this book would not be possible.
They believed in, and supported our dreams and raised
us to believe that anything is possible.*

TABLE OF CONTENTS

Preface 6

Basic Elements of Music 7
    Note Trees 7
    Table of Notes and Rests 8
    Dotted Note Values 8
    Dotted Rest Values 8
    Table of Dynamics 8
    Parts of the Staff 9

Equipment 10
    Getting Started 10
    DJ Setups 10
    Standard DJ Setup 10
    Battle DJ Setup 10
    Digital Vinyl System—Battle DJ Setup 11
    Parts of the Turntable 12
    Slipmats 13
    Parts of the Needle 14
    Headshell with Cartridge 14
    Headshell with Cartridge and Headshell Weight 14
    Parts of the Mixer 15

Marking the Record 16
    Battle Setup Marked at 12 O'clock 16
    Battle Setup Marked at Needle 16
    Standard Setup Marked at Needle 16

Hand Positions 17
    Standard Setup Clock 17
    Standard Setup Hand Placement 17
    Battle Setup Hand Placement 17

Fader Positions 18
    Closed Fader Position 18
    Open Fader Position 18

Suggestions on How to Practice 19

Message from the Authors 19

LESSONS 20

The "Baby Scratch" 20
    Lesson 1 20
    Lesson 2 22

Lesson 3	24
Lesson 4	26
Lesson 5—Playing Exercise 1	27
Lesson 6	29
Lesson 7	30
Lesson 8—Playing Exercise 2	31

The "Chirp" 32

Lesson 9	32
Lesson 10	34
Lesson 11—Playing Exercise 3	35
Lesson 12	36
Lesson 13	37
Lesson 14—Playing Exercise 4	38
Lesson 15	39
Lesson 16	40
Lesson 17—Playing Exercise 5	41
Lesson 18	42
Lesson 19	44
Lesson 20	45
Lesson 21	46
Lesson 22—Playing Exercise 6	47

The "Drop" 48

Lesson 23	48
Lesson 24	50

The "Cut" 51

Lesson 25	51
Lesson 26	52
Lesson 27	53
Lesson 28	54
Lesson 29—Playing Exercise 7	55
Lesson 30	56
Lesson 31	57
Lesson 32—Playing Exercise 8	58

Dynamics Drills 59

Drill 1	59
Drill 2	60
Drill 3	61

About the Authors 62

PREFACE

Scratching Made Easy Turntable Method Book 1: A Guide to Scratching is an elementary method book designed for the DJ. The aim of this book is to help you develop timing, dexterity, coordination, strength, rhythmic phrasing, quality of tone, and dynamics. With regular practice, you will be able to acquire these skills.

Over the years, we have observed numerous problems that a large number of Scratch DJs encounter. One of the most significant issues appears to be poor timing: In comparison to performances involving traditional instruments, such as the drums, bass, or keyboards, the playing of the Scratch DJ is often inconsistent with the selected music. This looks to be a result of a lack of understanding of time signatures and the basics of music theory.

However, there are highly skilled Scratch DJs that have been able to overcome this obstacle, despite the lack of educational resources.

Due to the scarcity of educational resources and the need for a learning process that leads to a high level of technical proficiency, *Turntable Method Book 1: A Guide to Scratching* has been created and designed to satisfy the demand.

BASIC ELEMENTS OF MUSIC

Note Trees

Note values in Binary time.

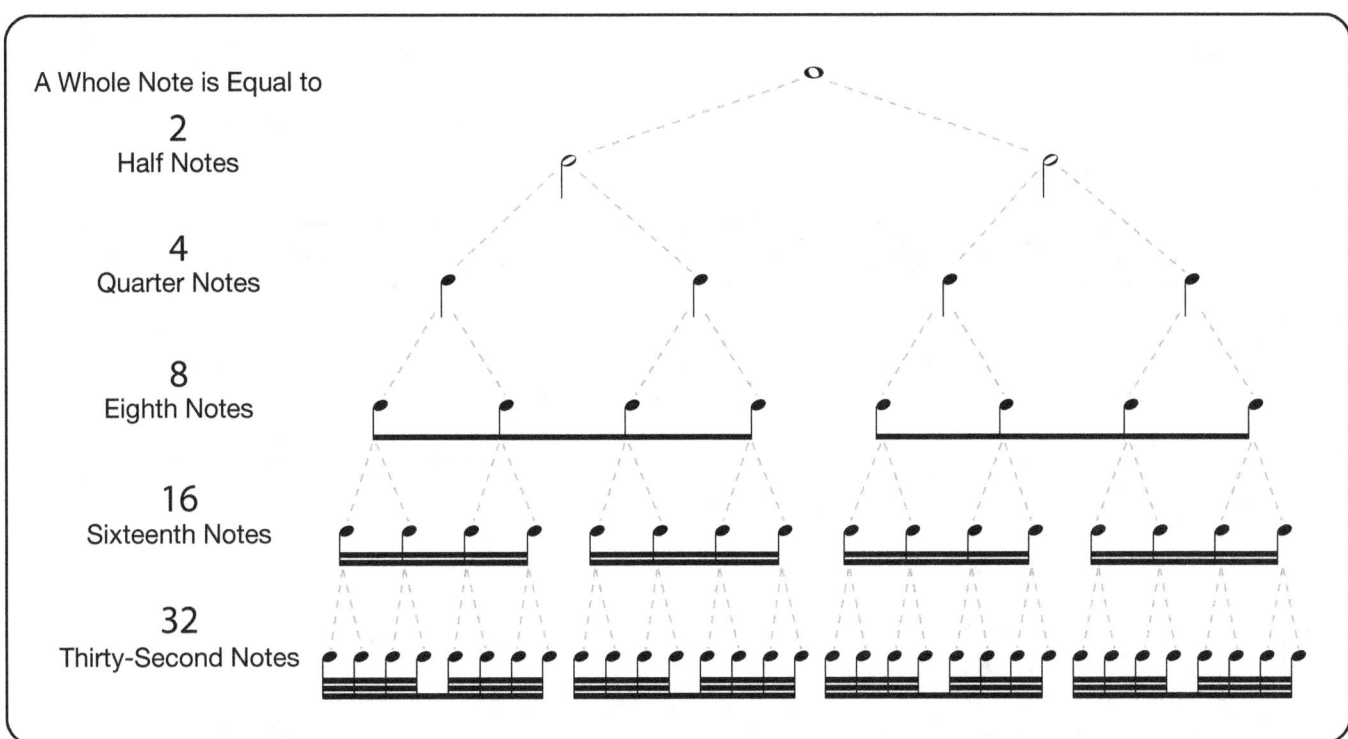

Note values in Ternary time.

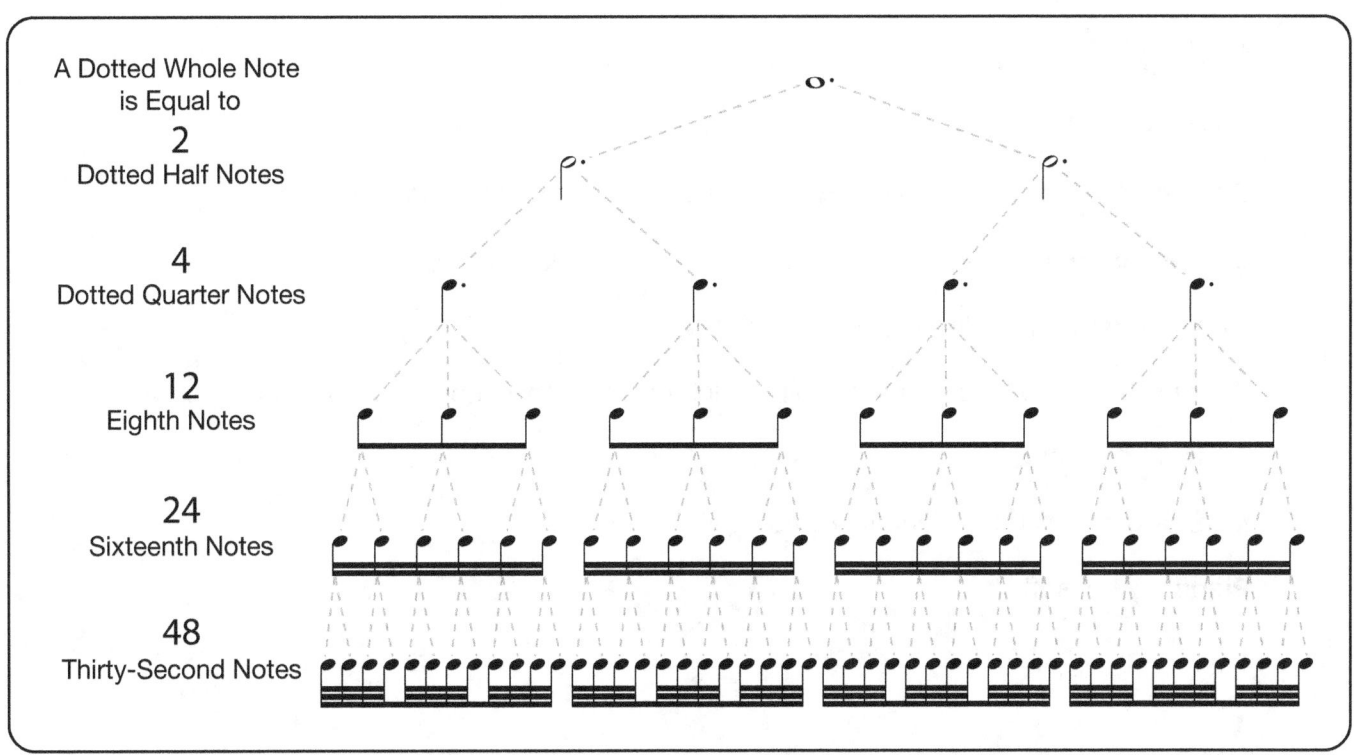

Table of Notes and Rests

	Whole	Half	Quarter	Eighth	Sixteenth	Thirty-Second
Note	𝅝	𝅗𝅥	♩	♪	𝅘𝅥𝅯	𝅘𝅥𝅰
Rest	𝄻	𝄼	𝄽	𝄾	𝄿	𝅀

Dotted Note Values

𝅝. = 𝅝 + 𝅗𝅥

𝅗𝅥. = 𝅗𝅥 + ♩

♩. = ♩ + ♪

♪. = ♪ + 𝅘𝅥𝅯

𝅘𝅥𝅯. = 𝅘𝅥𝅯 + 𝅘𝅥𝅰

Dotted Rest Values

𝄻. = 𝄻 + 𝄼

𝄼. = 𝄼 + 𝄽

𝄽. = 𝄽 + 𝄾

𝄾. = 𝄾 + 𝄿

𝄿. = 𝄿 + 𝅀

Table of Dynamics

Accent: (>) Strong attack

Crescendo (*Cresc.*) or ⎯⎯⎯⎯⎯⎯⎯⎯ increasing in loudness

Decrescendo (*Decresc.*) or ⎯⎯⎯⎯⎯⎯⎯⎯ decreasing in loudness

Diminuendo (*dim.*): decreasing in loudness

Dynamics: the loudness or volume in which notes, phrases, or compositions are played.

Forte (f): loud

Mezzo forte (mf): moderately loud

Piano (p): soft

Parts of the Staff

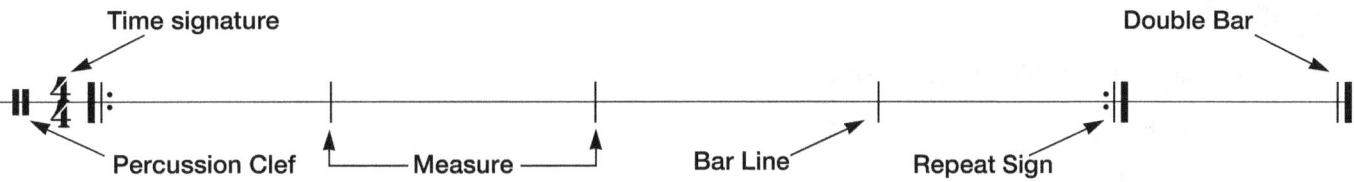

Percussion Clef:	Symbol located at the beginning of a staff that indicates percussion music.
Time Signature:	Numbers located on the staff that indicate the number of beats in a measure and the pulse of the song. The top number determines the number of beats in a measure. The bottom number determines what note gets the beat. For example, 4/4 means the beat is in quarter notes and there are 4 beats in a measure.
Measure:	Organizes music into sections that contain a designated number of beats.
Bar Line:	Separates measures.
Repeat Sign:	Indicates what section is to be repeated. This can be either from the beginning of the piece or a section between two repeat signs.
Double Bar:	Marks the conclusion of a piece of music.

EQUIPMENT

Getting Started

- Needle (Headshell and Cartridge)
- Slipmats
- Headphones
- Playback system, i.e., amps and speakers
- Vinyl records or a Digital Vinyl System (DVS) and computer

DJ Setups

Figure 1 • Standard DJ setup

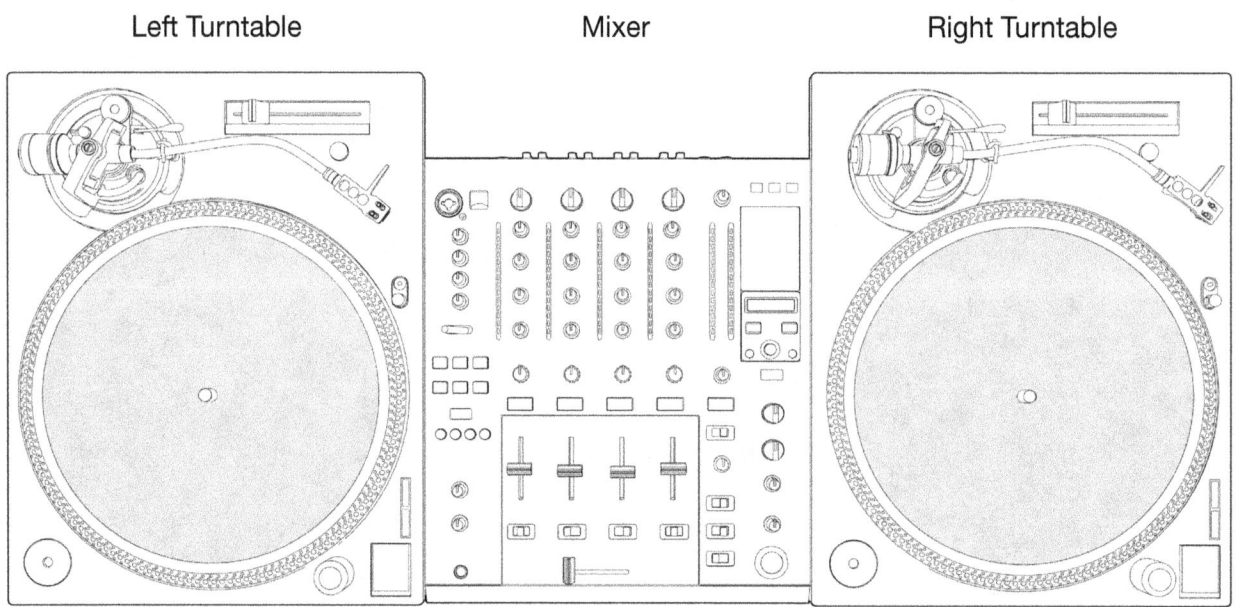

Figure 2 • Battle DJ setup

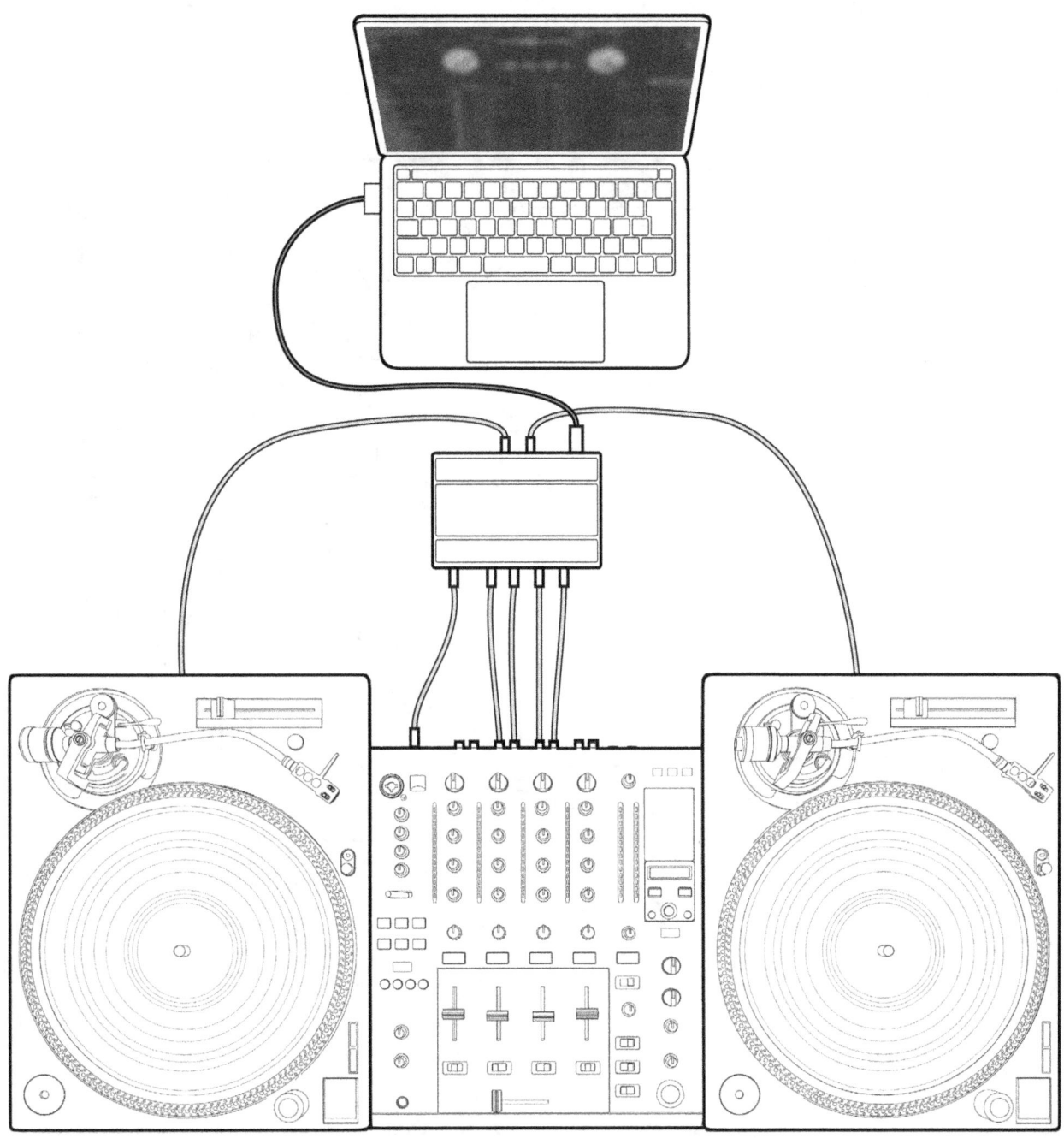

Figure 3 • Digital Vinyl System—Battle DJ Setup

Parts of the Turntable

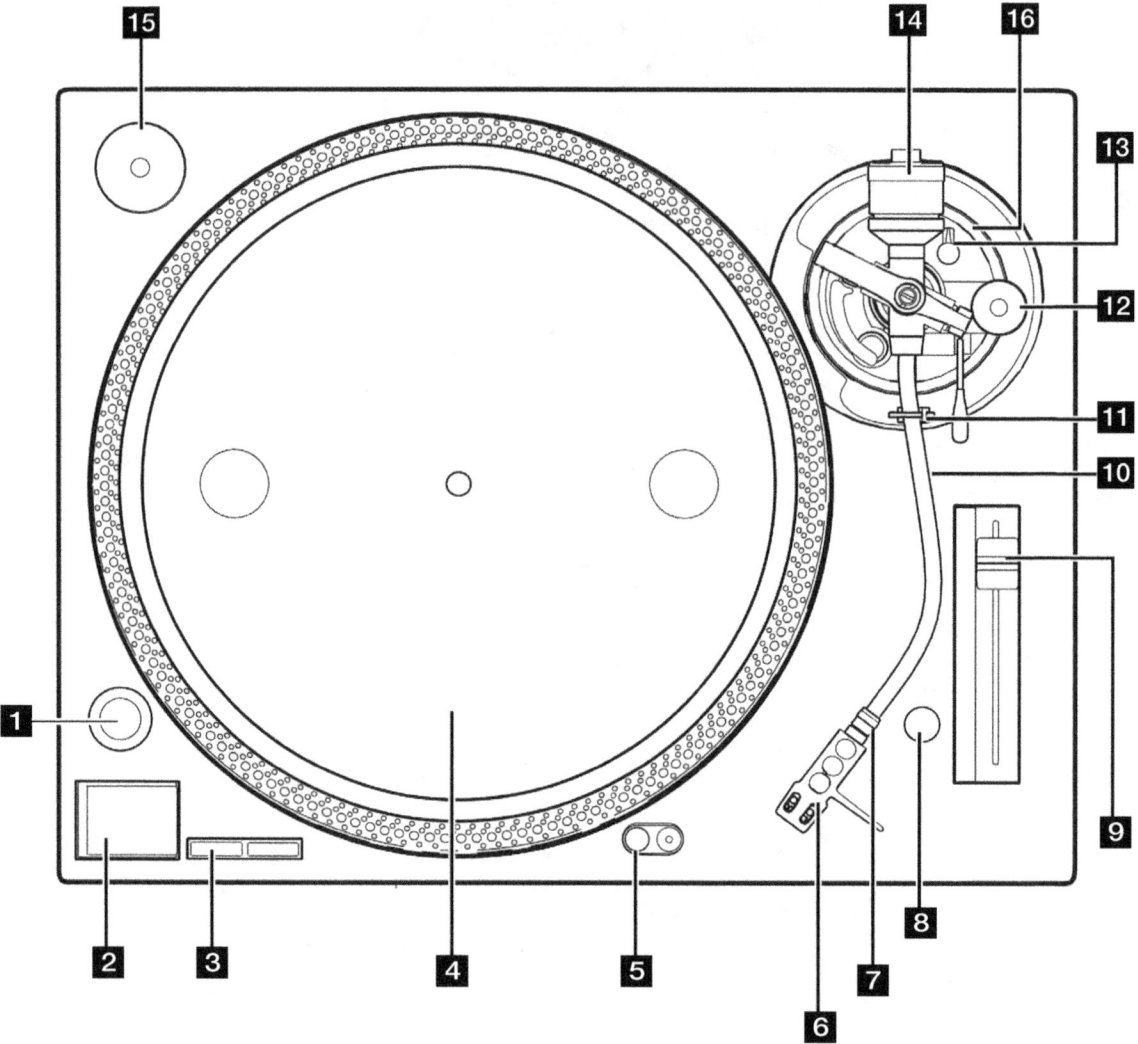

Figure 4 • Turntable

1 **ON/OFF**
Supplies power to the turntable.

2 **Start-Stop Button**
Pushing this button makes the turntable platter start of stop.

3 **Speed Change Buttons**
Determines the speed at which the turntable platter rotates.
- 33 1/3 rpm
- 45 rpm

4 **Turntable Platter**
The surface that the record is placed on.

5 **Stylus Illuminator**
Provides light for the stylus/needle.

6 **Headshell**
Holds the cartridge and stylus/needle assembly.

7 **Headshell Lock**
Locking nut that keeps the headshell in place.

8 **Tempo Rest Button**
When on the turntable platter will rotate at the determined speed (33 1/3 rpm or 45 rpm) regardless of the position of the tempo control.

9 **Tempo Control**
Slides up and down and allows you to adjust the speed of the turntable platter.

10 **Tone Arm**
Holds the headshell and cartridge.

11 **Arm Clamp**
Holds down the tonearm.

12 **Anti-Skating Control**
Prevents the stylus/needle from skating when a record is being played.

13 **Arm Height Lock**
Locks the height of the tonearm.

14 **Balance Weight**
Balances the tonearm and regulates the pressure on the stylus.

15 **EP Record Adapter**
Insert that allows standard EP records to be played.

16 **Arm-Height Adjustment**
Adjusts the tonearm height.

Slipmats

Slipmats allow for easier manipulation of the record.

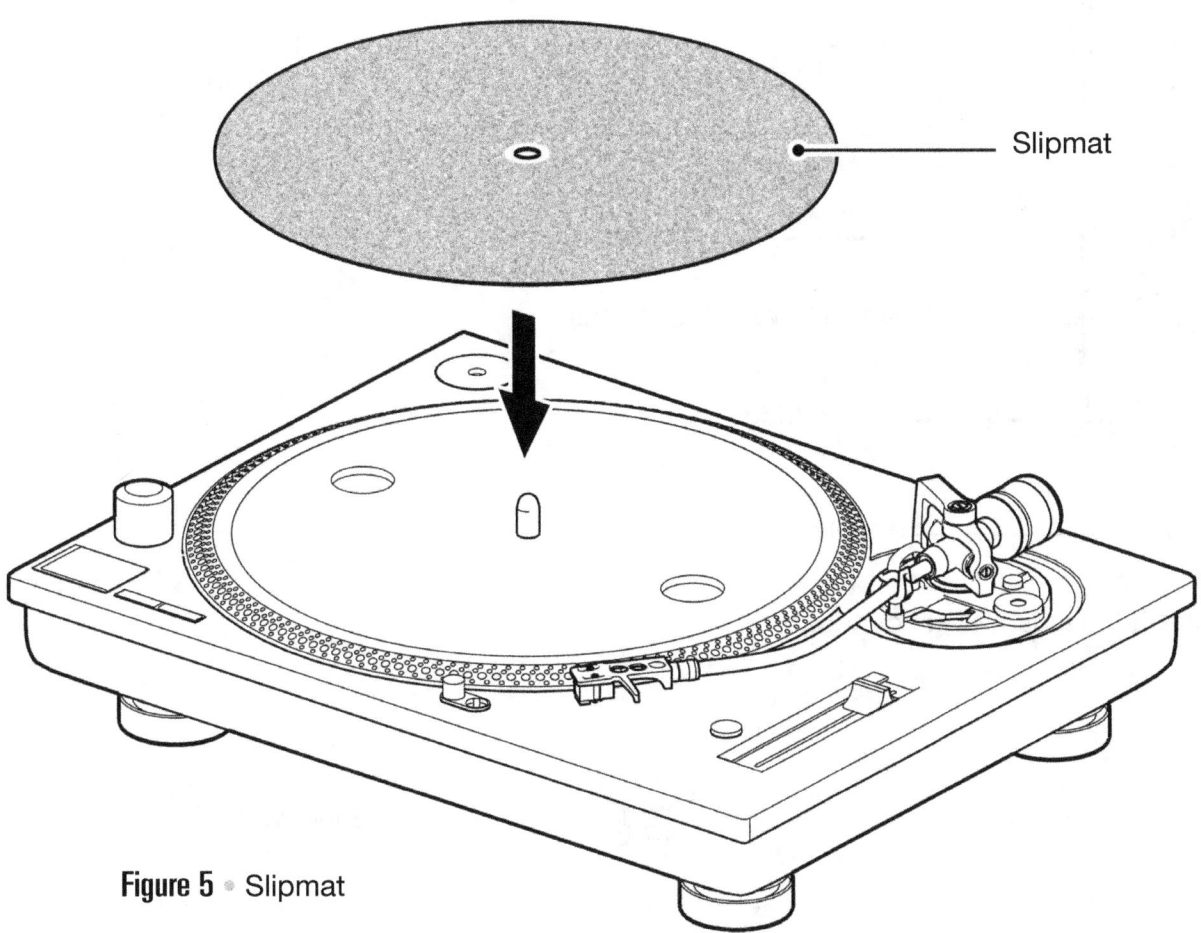

Figure 5 • Slipmat

Parts of the Needle

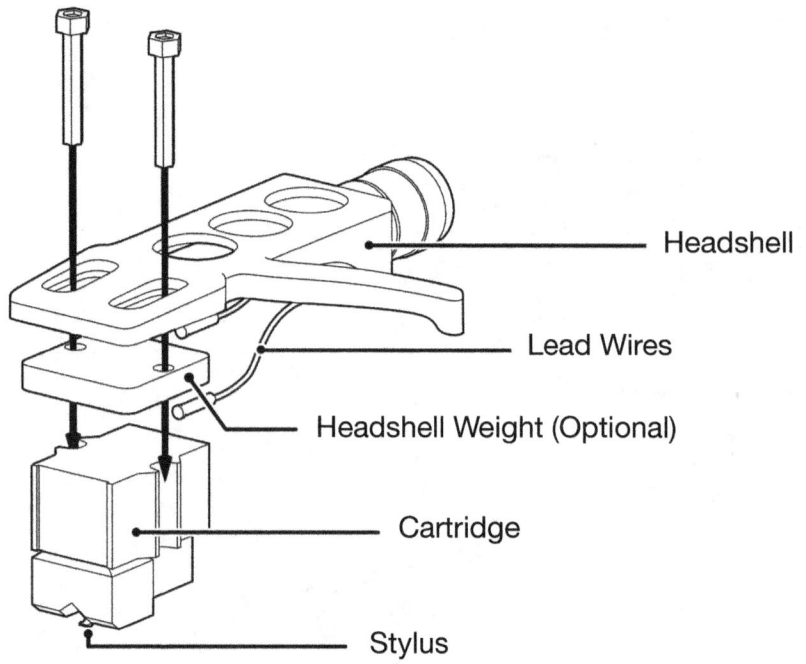

Figure 6 • Headshell with cartridge

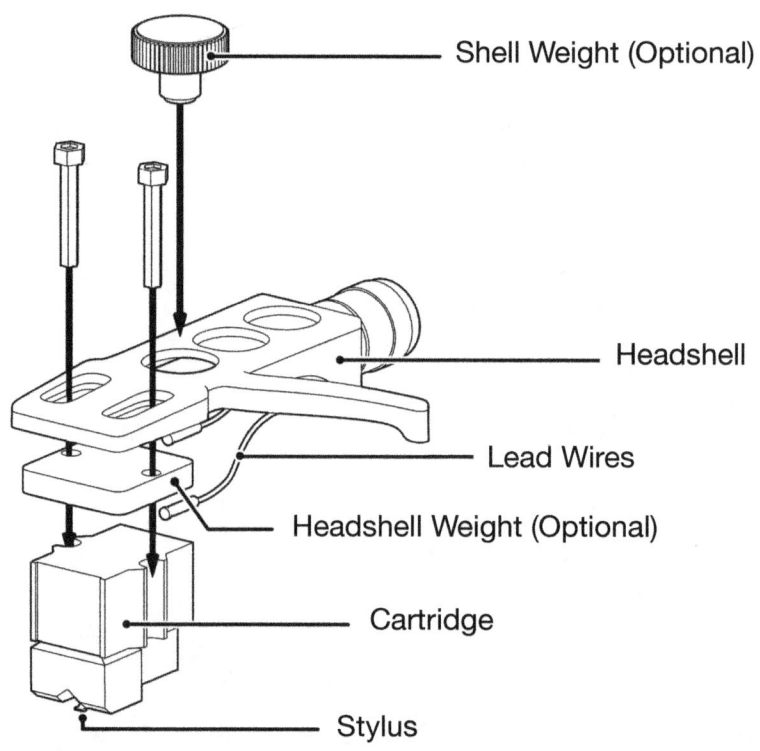

Figure 7 • Headshell with cartridge and headshell weight

Parts of the Mixer

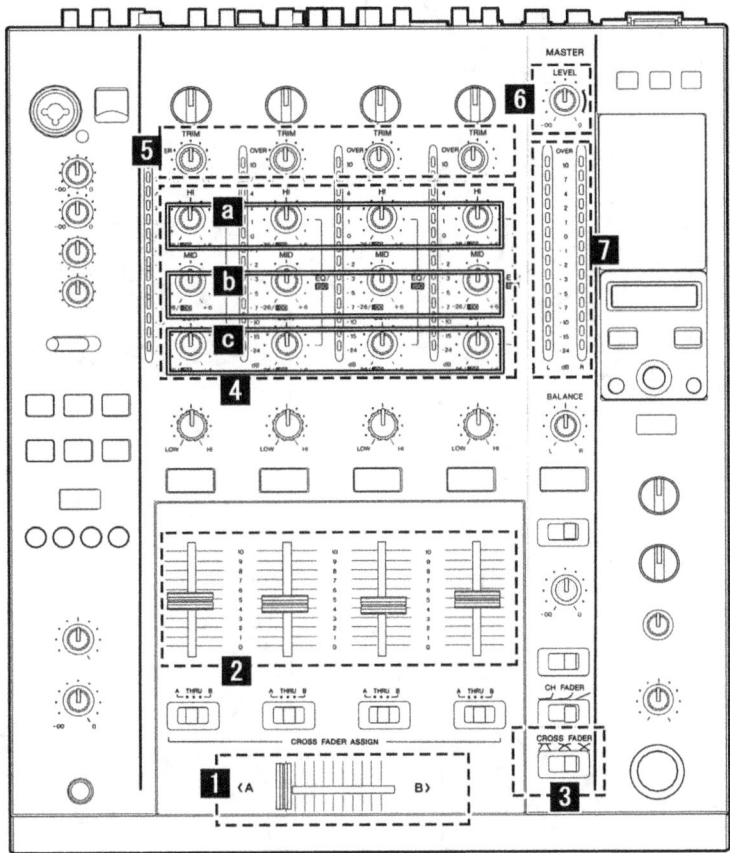

Figure 8 • Mixer

1 Cross Fader
Use the cross fader to mix between the active channels

2 Channel Fader
Adjusts the audio volume level output of the channel

3 Cross Fader Slope Selector (ㄇ ㄨ ㄨ)
Changes the cross fader slope characteristics

4 Equalizer
Boosts or cuts the output of the high, mid, low range frequencies
   a) High
   b) Mid
   c) Low

5 Gain/Trim
Adjusts the input of audio level to each channel

6 Master Volume
Adjusts the audio volume level of the master output

7 Master Volume Level
The LEDs display the audio level of the master

Marking of the Record

Records are often marked with stickers that indicate cue points or the position of a sound. Records are generally marked at 12 o'clock or at the stylus/needle.

Use this as a reference to identify the location of sounds.

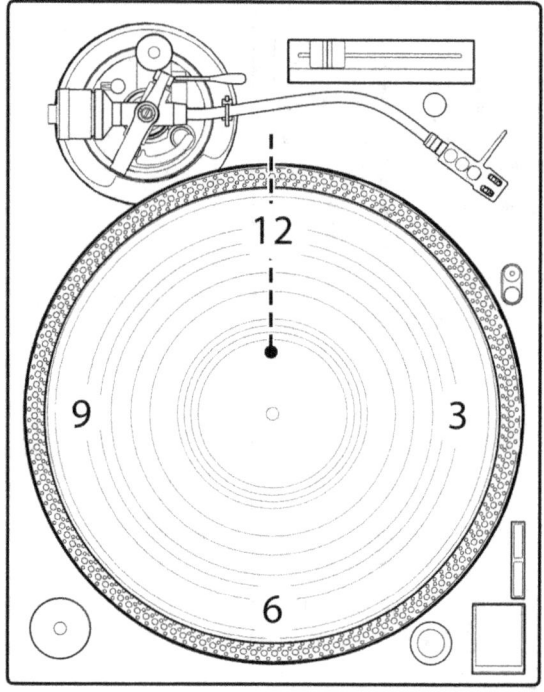

Figure 9 • Battle setup marked at 12 o'clock

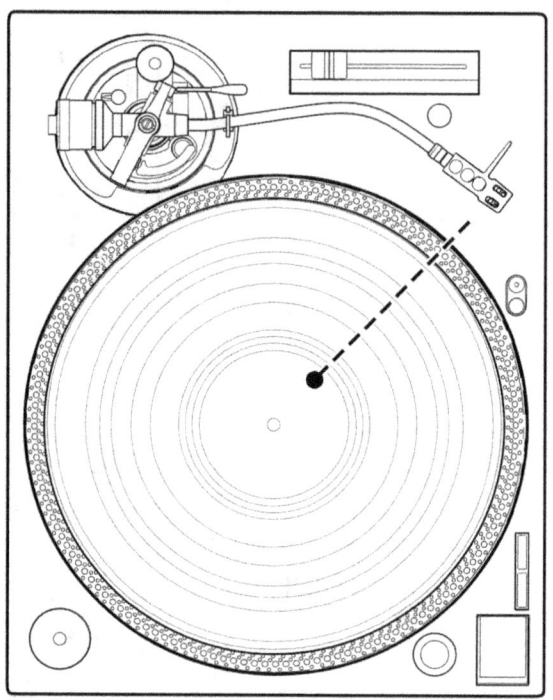

Figure 10 • Battle setup marked at needle

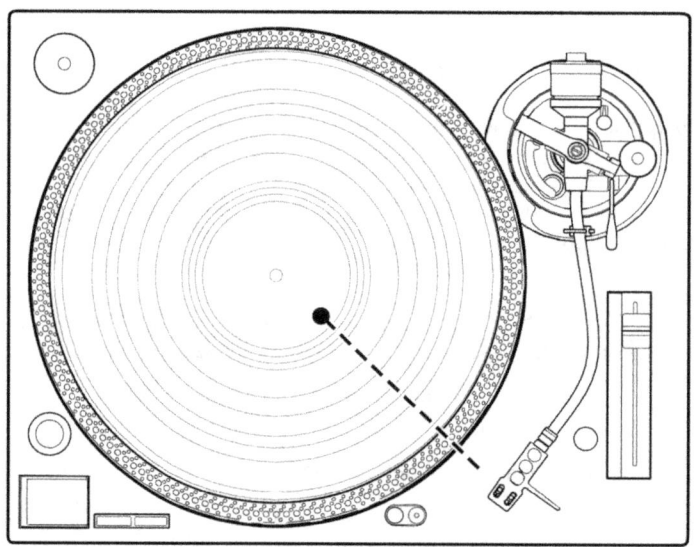

Figure 11 • Standard setup marked at needle

HAND POSITIONS

Generally, hands are placed between 9 o'clock and 11 o'clock. Choose a comfortable position that prevents you from hitting the tone arm.

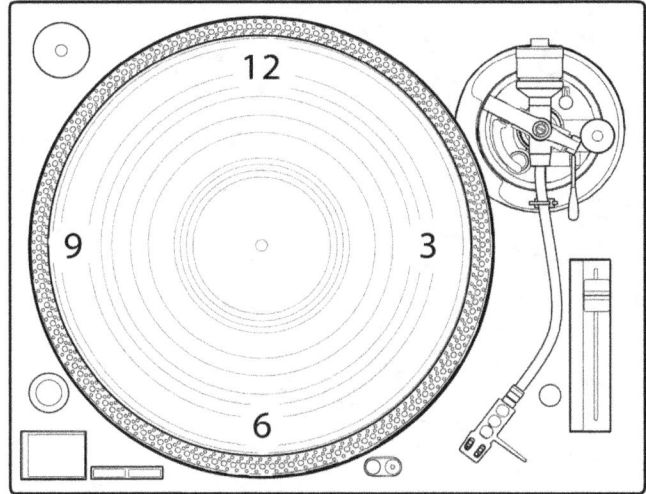

Figure 12 • Standard setup clock

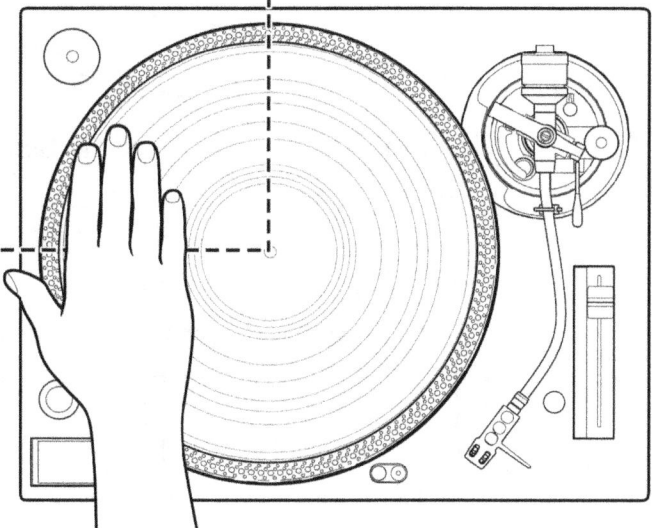

Figure 13 • Standard setup hand placement

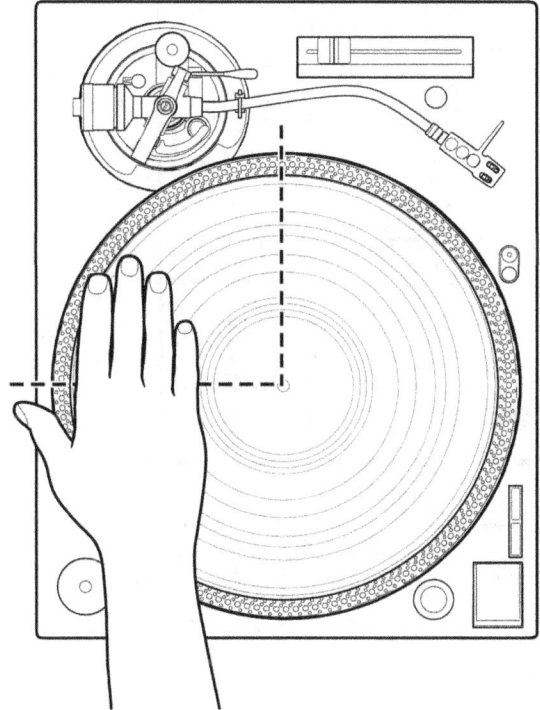

Figure 14 • Battle setup hand placement

FADER POSITIONS

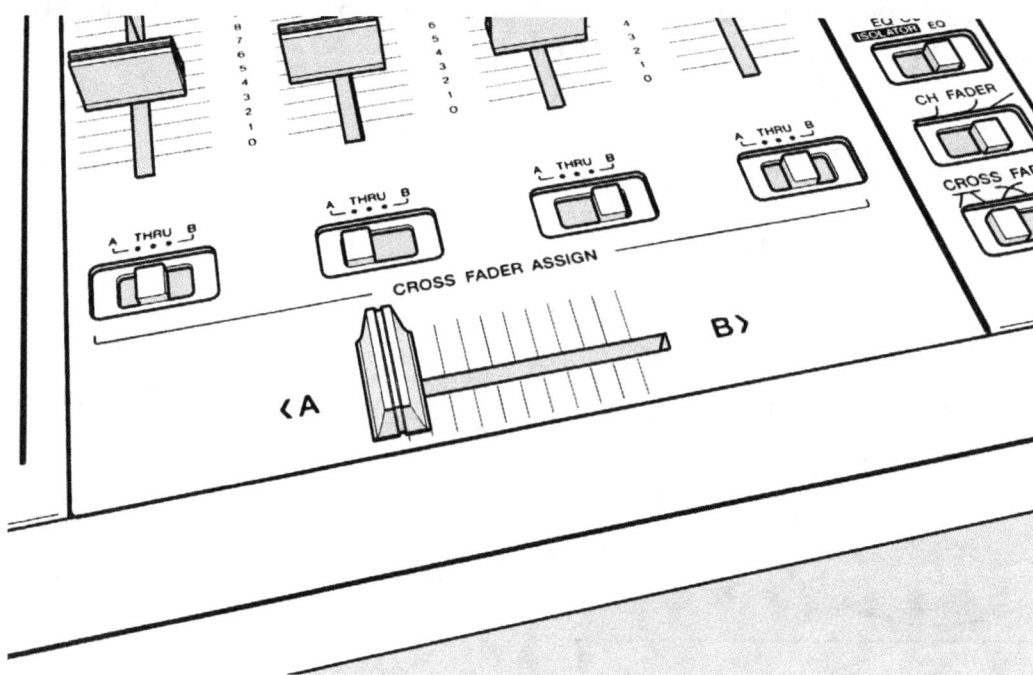

Figure 15 • Closed fader position. Side B emits no sound.

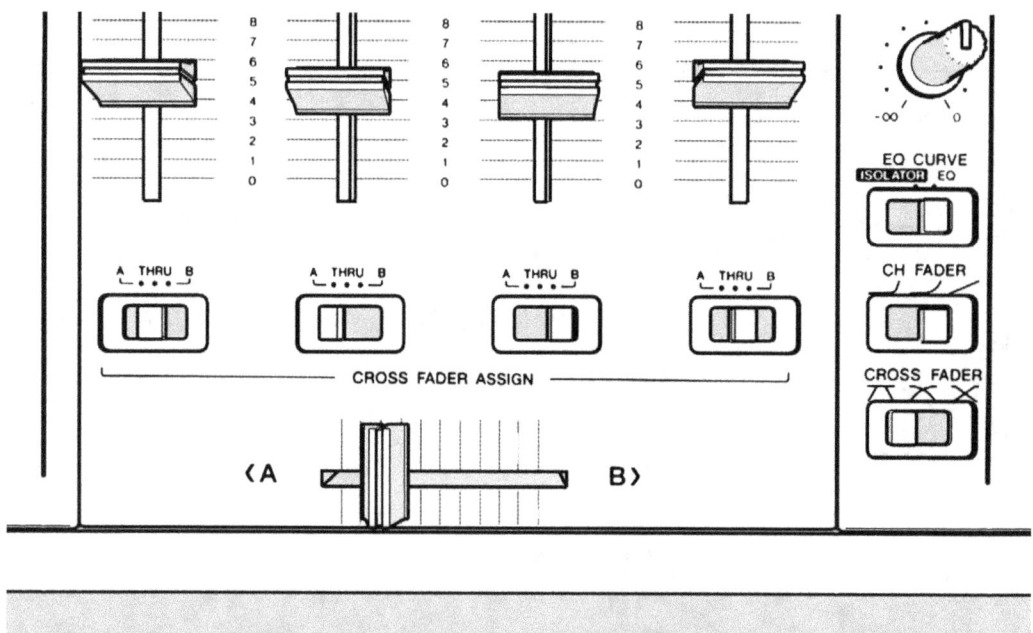

Figure 16 • Open fader position.

SUGGESTIONS ON HOW TO PRACTICE

1. Count out loud.

2. Practice at different tempos varying from slow to fast.

3. Allocate some of your practice time to playing with a metronome, not just performing with your favorite music.

4. Practice each lesson with both hands. A great deal of time and effort is required to achieve ambidexterity.

5. Keep your body relaxed. Resist the natural urge to tighten your muscles.

6. Play the music as written. Endeavor to play each lesson without errors before proceeding to the next page.

7. Improvisation is an integral part of scratching and it is the process of creating music on the spot. It is a skill that is learned and developed over time. Use the rhythms in this book as guides to create different variations. Dedicate time to improvisation and incorporate what you have learned into your practice sessions. An ideal time to practice improvisation would be after each Playing Exercise.

MESSAGE FROM THE AUTHORS

Exceptional performance is acquired by means of routine practice. It is best to practice as often as possible. A little practice every day is better than a lot of practice once a week.

Note to the reader: All lessons are to be played with the turntable *on* — meaning, the turntable platter should be revolving.

The "speed select" button should be set to 33 rpm.

For the best results set your fader select to: (⊼)

LESSONS

THE "BABY SCRATCH"

Lesson 1

Lesson 1 is in 4/4 time, and the cross fader is to remain in the open position. In 4/4 time there are four beats in a measure, and a quarter note (♩) gets one beat. This lesson also contains the quarter rest (𝄽), which also gets one beat. Notice the markings for hand position: F = forward hand stroke and B = backward hand stroke. Count out loud while playing, keep an even tempo, and observe the repeat signs (‖: :‖).

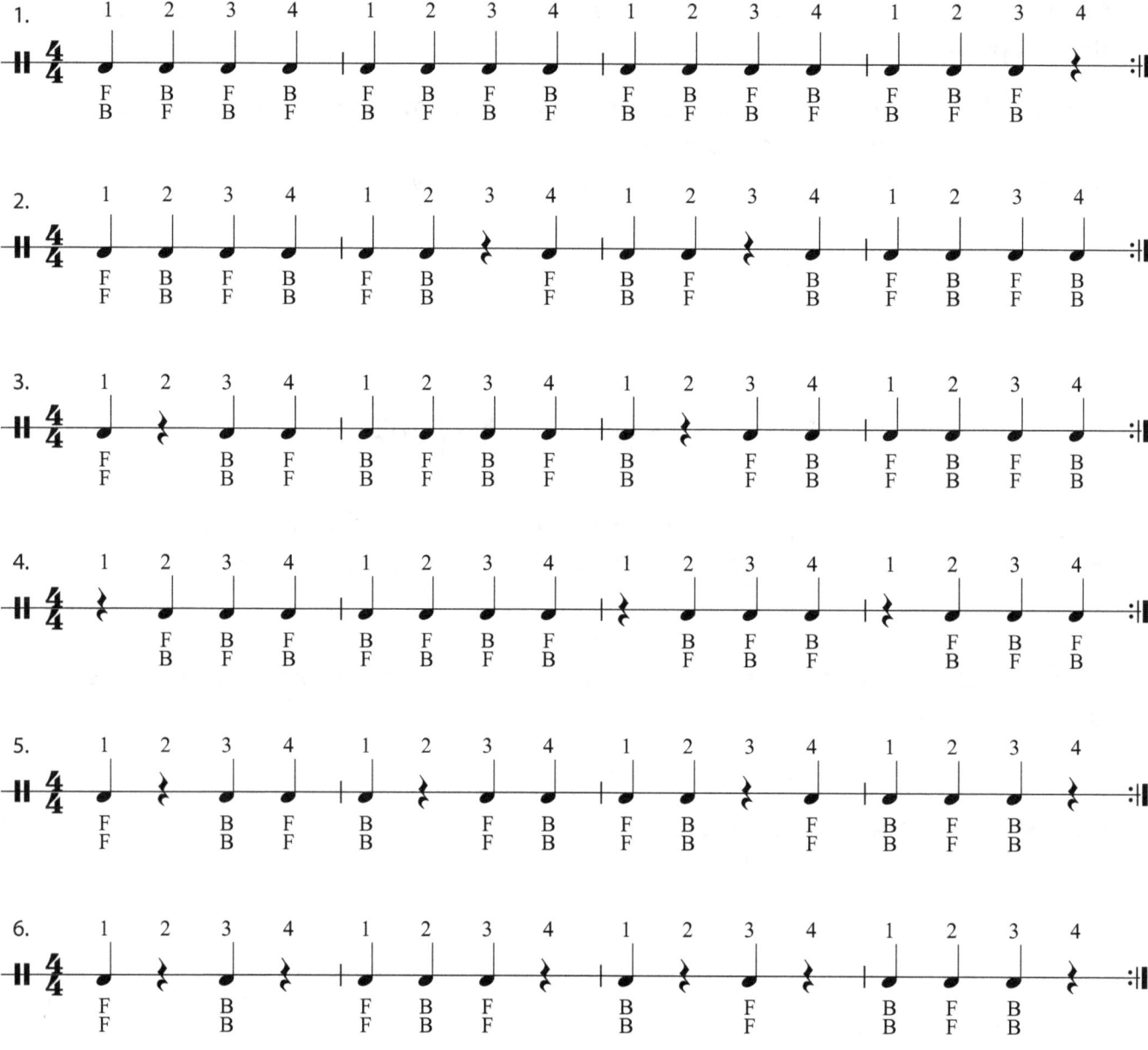

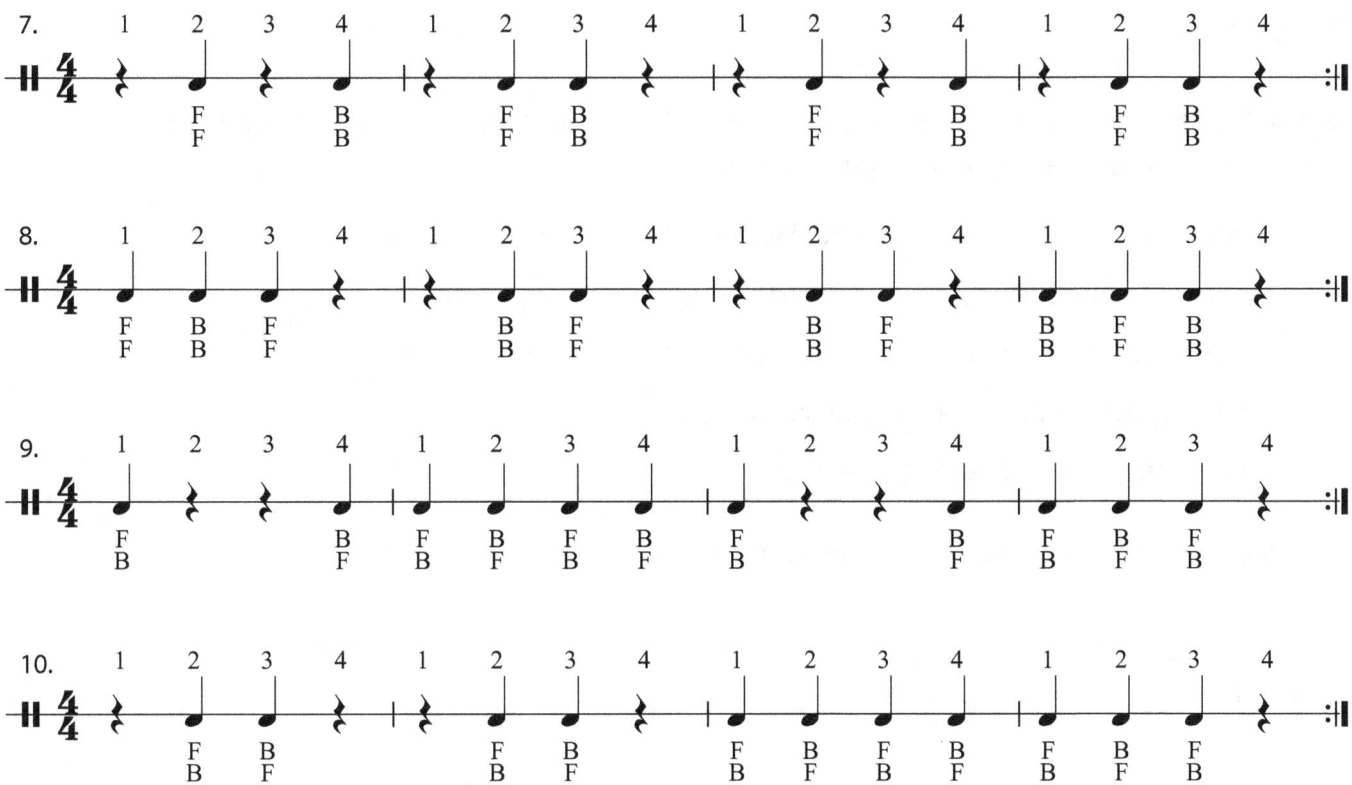

Lesson 2

Lesson 2 introduces whole notes (o), whole rests (-), half notes (𝅗𝅥), and half rests (-).
The following notes and rests are equal in value:

- Whole notes and whole rests equal four beats: o and - = 4 beats.
- Half notes and half rests equal two beats: 𝅗𝅥 and - = 2 beats.
- Quarter notes and quarter rests equal one beat: ♩ and 𝄽 = 1 beat.
- Whole notes o are to be played as: ♩ 𝄽 𝄽 𝄽
- Half notes 𝅗𝅥 are to be played as: ♩ 𝄽

Continue to count out loud and keep an even tempo.

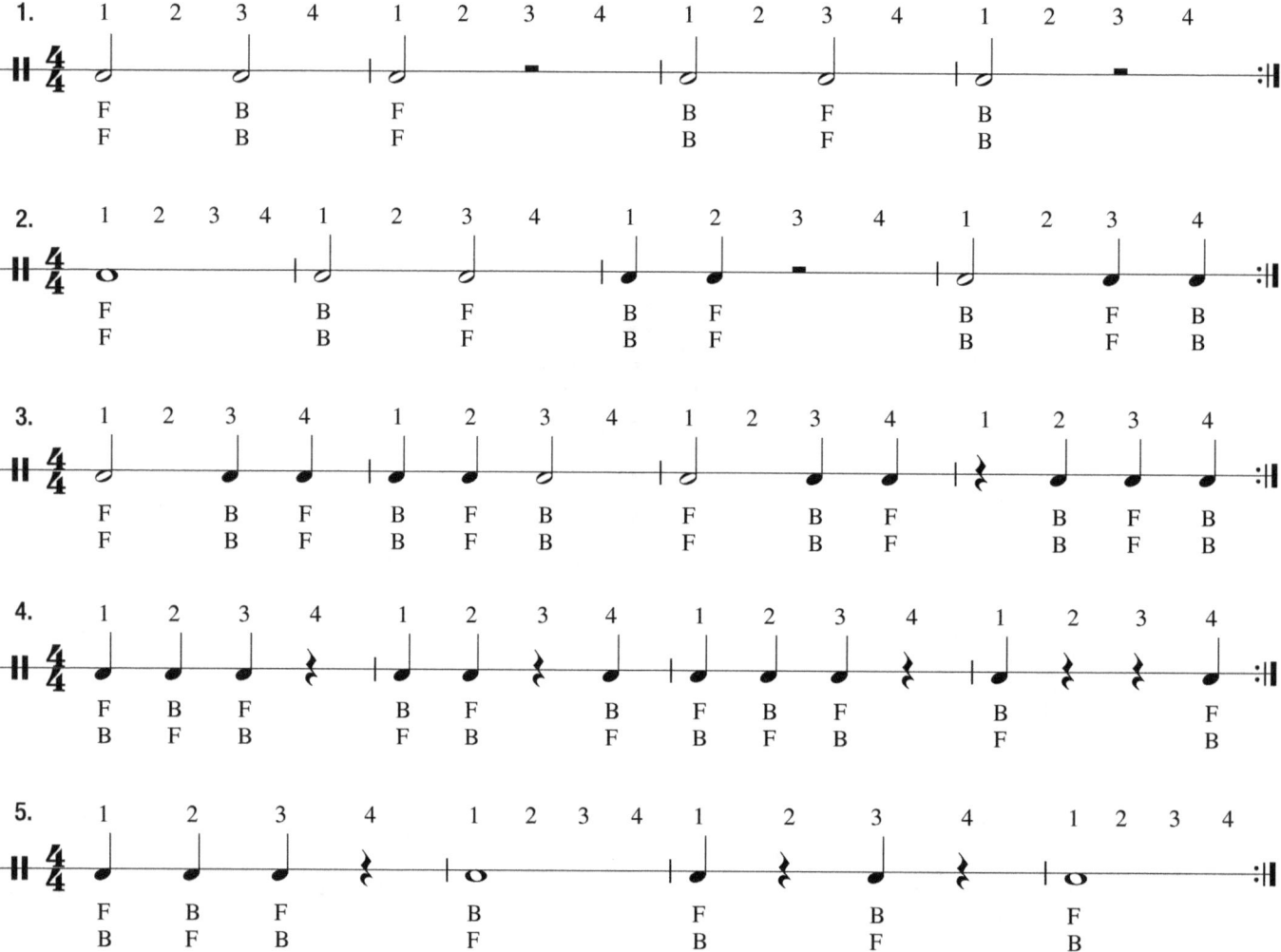

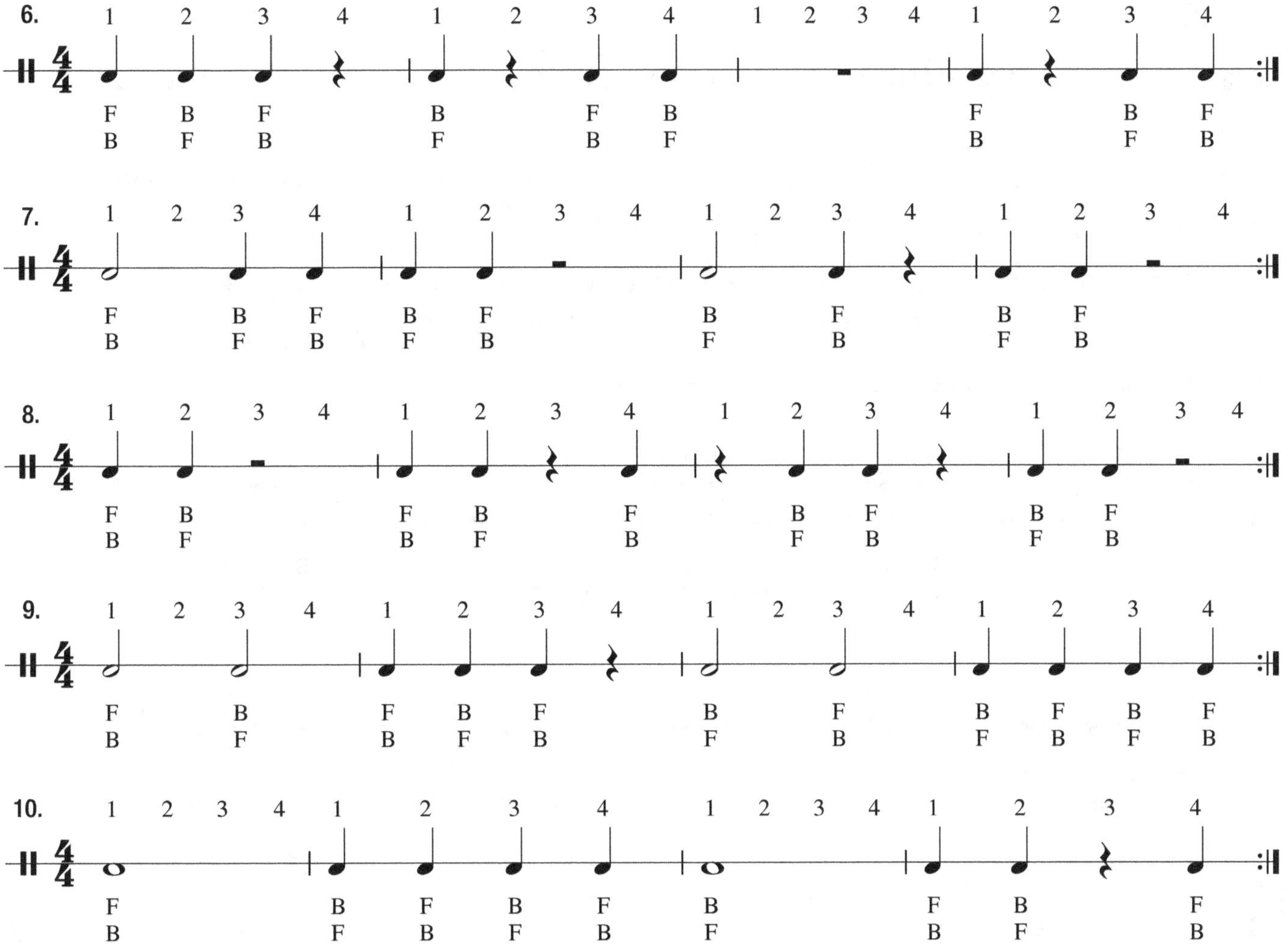
6.
1 2 3 4 1 2 3 4 1 2 3 4 1 2 3 4
F B F B F B F B F
B F B F B F B F B
7.
1 2 3 4 1 2 3 4 1 2 3 4 1 2 3 4
F B F B F B F B F
B F B F B F B F B
8.
1 2 3 4 1 2 3 4 1 2 3 4 1 2 3 4
F B F B F B F B F
B F B F B F B F B
9.
1 2 3 4 1 2 3 4 1 2 3 4 1 2 3 4
F B F B F B F B F B F
B F B F B F B F B F B
10.
1 2 3 4 1 2 3 4 1 2 3 4 1 2 3 4
F B F B F B F B F
B F B F B F B F B

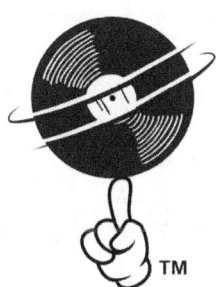

Lesson 3

Lesson 3 introduces the eighth note (♪). Now you're getting into faster notes for increased tempo.

- The value of an eighth note is half the value of a quarter note. This means two eighth notes (♪♪) equal one quarter note (♩).
- When consecutive eighth notes are written, they are joined together by a "beam" (♫). Eighth notes are counted as "one & two & three & four &".
- Continue to count out loud and keep an even tempo.

25

Lesson 4

Lesson 4 is a continuation of the previous exercise, adding more varied quarter and eighth note patterns. Count out loud and maintain an even tempo.

Lesson 5 – Playing Exercise 1

This lesson consists of two pieces that are "Playing Exercises." These pieces incorporate previously covered material.

Here is an introduction to accents (>) and other dynamics (*p*-*f*, *cresc.*). Play the accented notes with slightly more emphasis. The accented note should be played louder and will have a higher pitch. After completing this exercise, incorporate these rhythms into your improvisation practice.

- Accents (>) over a note indicate a stronger attack.
- Piano (*p*) has a lighter attack and forte (*f*) has a stronger attack.
- A mezzo forte (*mf*) attack is stronger than a piano but softer than a forte attack.
- A *crescendo* is a gradual increase in loudness. For the crescendo, gradually increase the strength of the attack. There are no repeat signs at the end of each line.

27

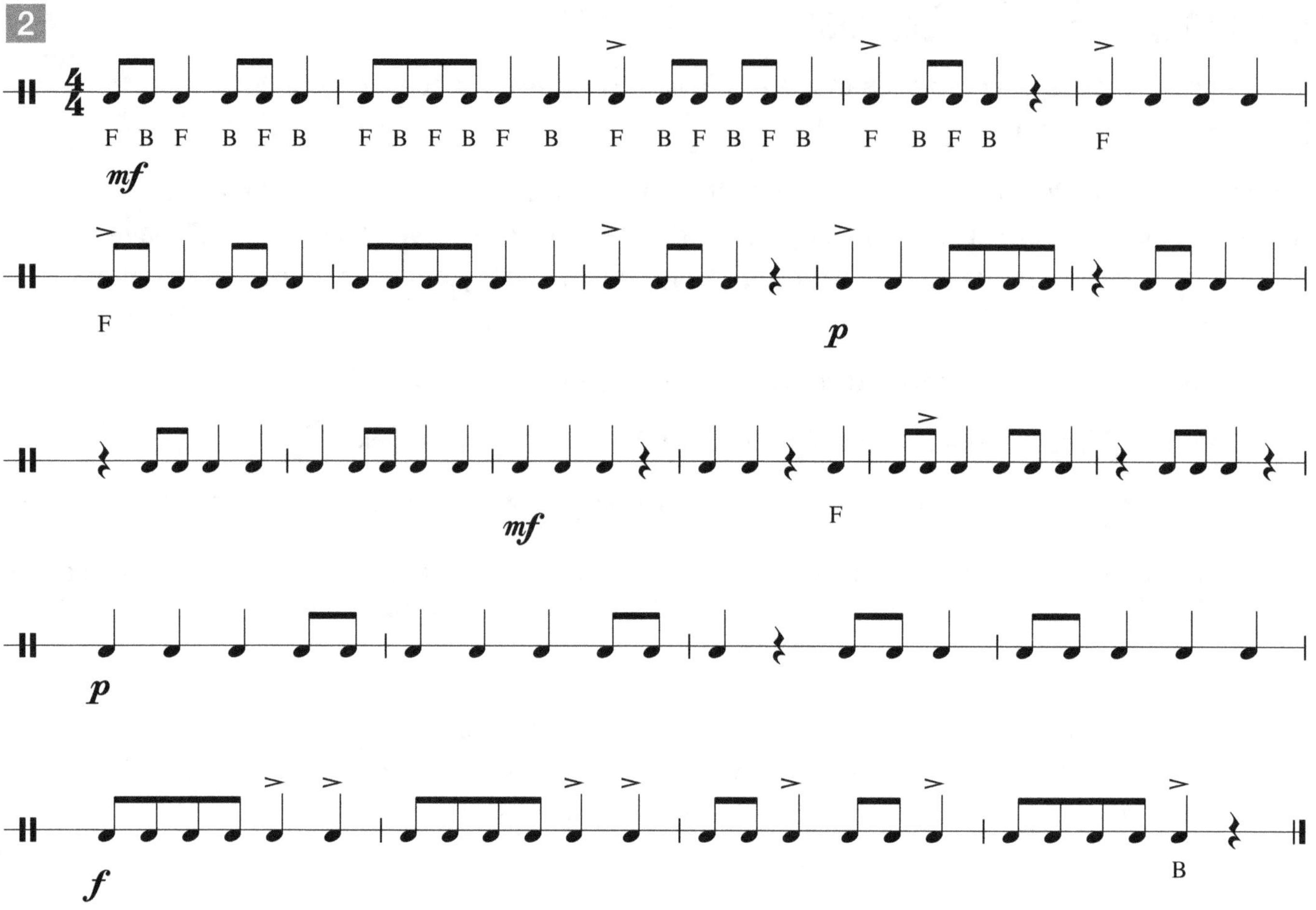
2
F B F B F B F B F B F B F B F B F B F B F B F
mf
F
p
mf
F
p
f
B

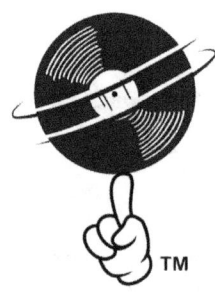

Lesson 6

In Lesson 6, to correspond with the eighth notes, here's the eighth rest (𝄾). The eighth rest and the eighth note have the same value (𝄾 = ♪). Two eighth rests equal one quarter rest (𝄾 𝄾 = 𝄽).

Lesson 7

Here's a more challenging focus on eighth notes and eighth rests.

Lesson 8 — Playing Exercise 2

Next, these two Playing Exercises incorporate all of the previously covered material and introduce the measure repeat sign. The measure repeat symbol (𝄎) indicates that the previously played measure is to be repeated. Note that the counting and strokes have been intentionally omitted to challenge you. And, there are no repeat signs at the end of each line. Play the dynamics as written and continue to count out loud.

THE "CHIRP"

Lesson 9

In this section you'll learn how to incorporate the *cross fader*.

A cross fader is a slide control on a mixer for fading in one channel while simultaneously fading out another. For best results for scratching, set your fader select to: (⊼)

This shortens the slope and allows the sound to be heard as soon as the fader is opened.

Begin with the cross fader in the open position.
- As you execute the forward stroke, quickly close the cross fader after hearing the sound.
- After properly completing the technique, your hand will be in the forward position and the cross fader will be closed.

From this position you will do the same thing in reverse.
- Quickly open the cross fader as you perform the backward stroke and close the cross fader after hearing the sound.
- After properly completing this technique, the fader will be in the closed position.
- When these techniques are completed consecutively, they are referred to commonly as the "chirp."

Apply these techniques to the rhythms below. Continue to count out loud and maintain an even tempo.

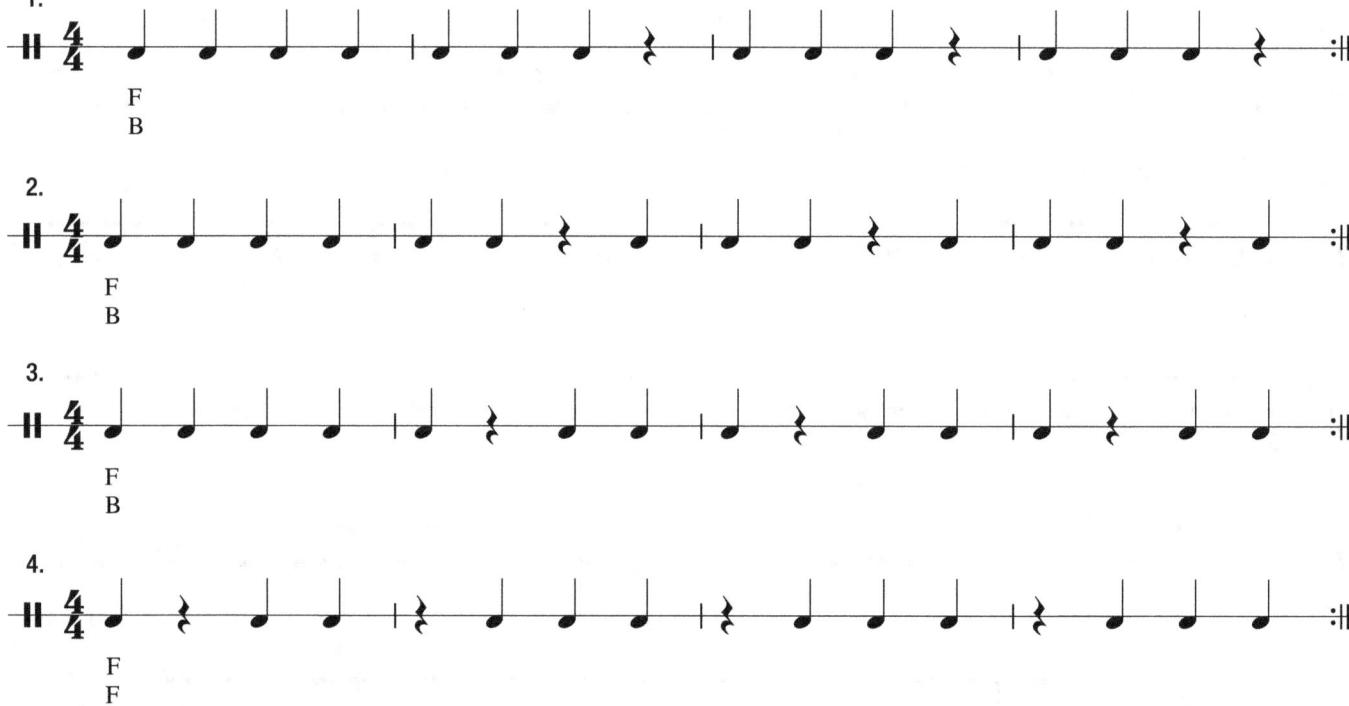

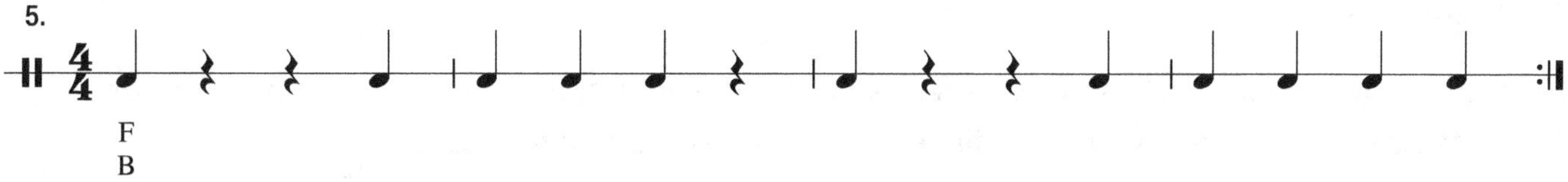

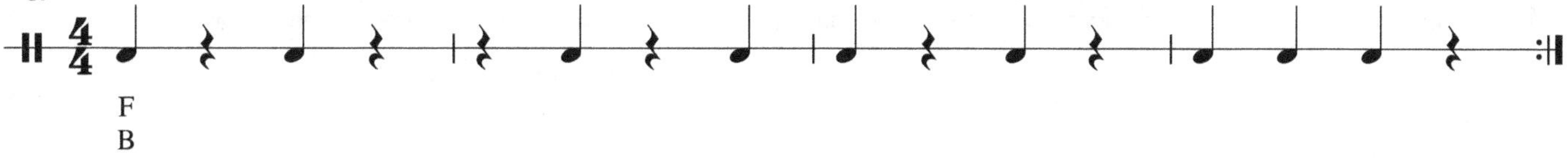

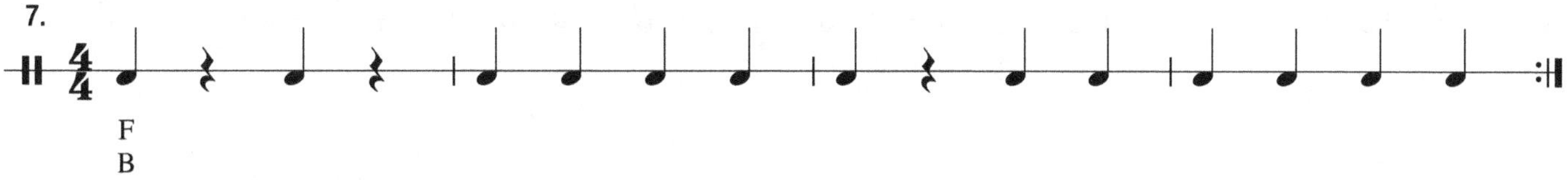

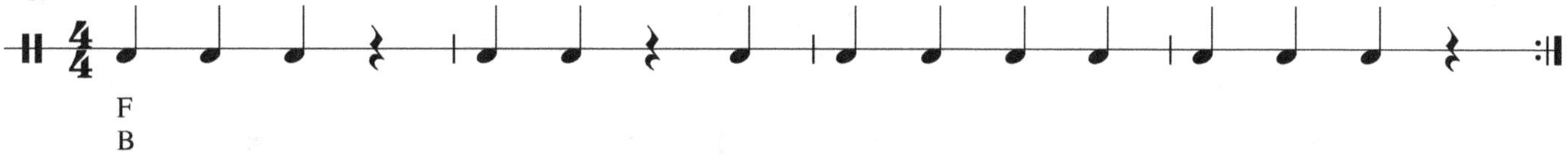

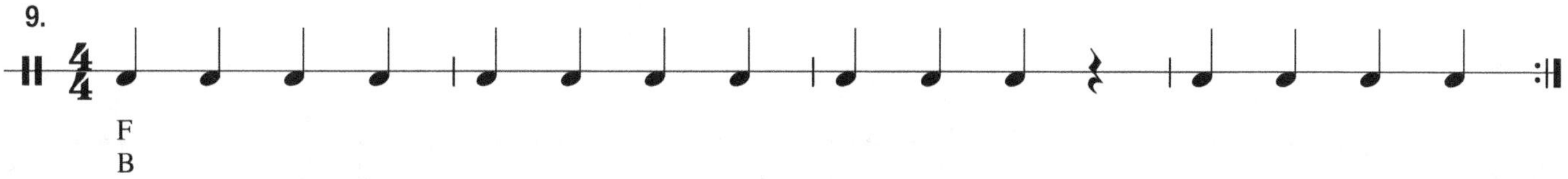

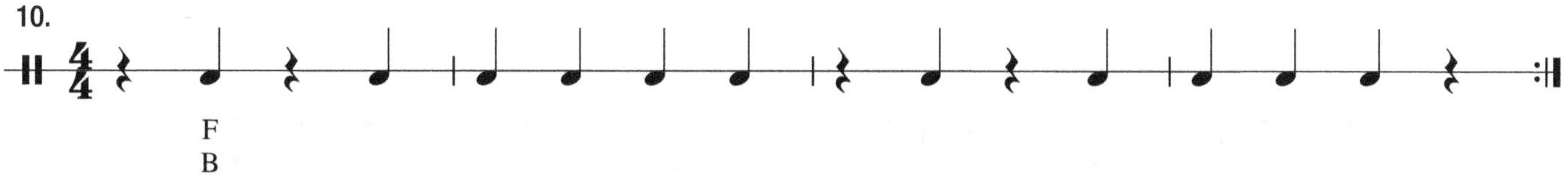

Lesson 10

Here is a continuation of the previous exercise with the addition of eighth notes and half notes. Plus, the use of the cross fader is continued. Each line should be repeated.

Lesson 11 – Playing Exercise 3

Here are two more Playing Exercises. Continue to use the cross fader with the rhythms provided below.

Lesson 12

In this exercise, open and closed fader techniques are combined. When notes are marked with a slur (⌣), the first and last note under the slur are played with an open fader. Where there is no slur, the fader should be used to create separation between notes, as you have done in previous exercises. The slur allows you to clearly indicate transitions between open and closed fader techniques.

Lesson 13

Now, continue the study of open and closed fader techniques, with the addition of eighth rests.

Lesson 14 – Playing Exercise 4

Here are two Playing Exercises that cover previous material.

Lesson 15

Introducing some new time signatures and rhythms now for Lesson 15. First, here's 6/8 time.

- In 6/8 time there are six beats in each measure, and the eighth note gets one beat.
- When playing in 6/8 there is a natural accent on beats 1 and 4.

And, here are the dotted quarter note and the dotted half note:

- One dotted quarter note gets three beats.
- One dotted half note gets six beats.

While counting out loud, execute clean and even strokes. There is a natural accent on beats 1 and 4. Make note not to overemphasize them.

Lesson 16

This is a continuation of using open and closed fader techniques. The counting and strokes have been purposely omitted to challenge you to do it yourself.

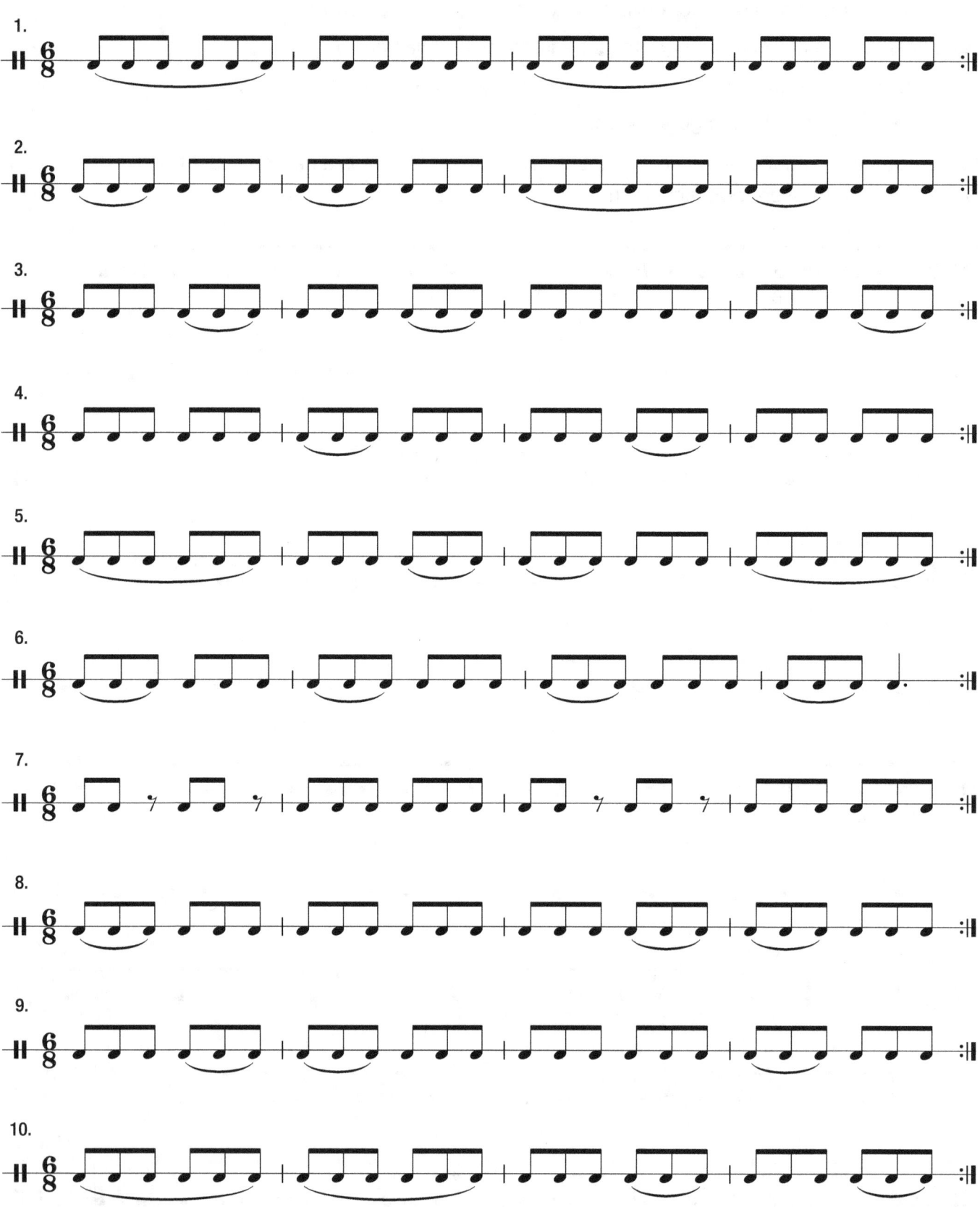

Lesson 17 — Playing Exercise 5

Here are two Playing Exercises that incorporate the use of the cross fader. Practice this lesson slowly at first and observe the accents. You'll need to concentrate to play the accents with an even tone.

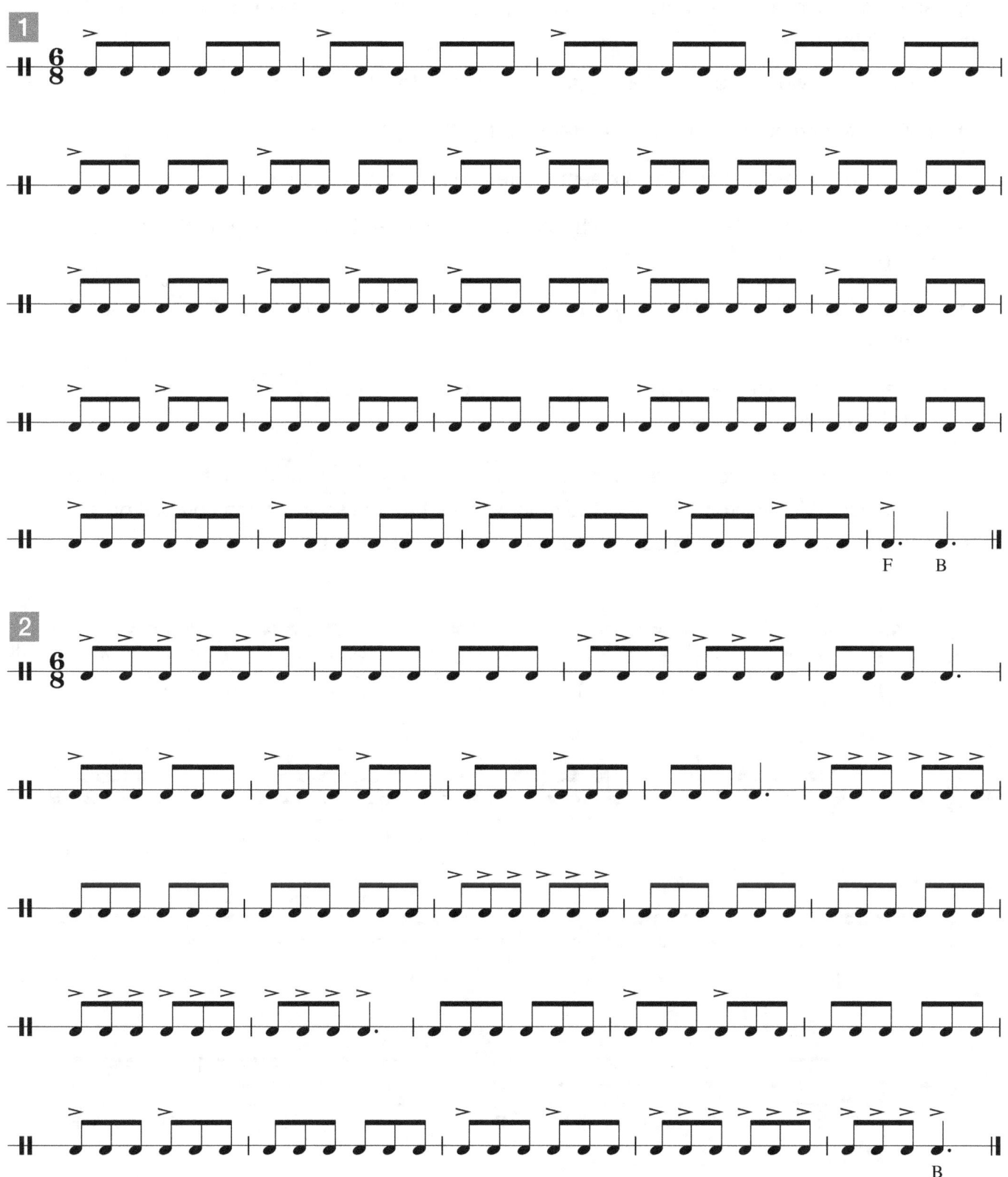

Lesson 18

Introducing 2/4 time.

- In 2/4 time there are two beats in a measure, and the quarter note gets one beat.

And, also introducing sixteenth notes (♬) and rests (𝄽). The value of a sixteenth note is half the value of an eighth note.

- This means two sixteenth notes equal one eighth note (♬♬ = ♪).
- Four sixteenth notes equal one quarter note (♬♬♬♬ = ♩).
- The sixteenth rest (𝄽) and the sixteenth note (♬) have the same value.
- Two sixteenth rests equal one eighth rest (𝄽𝄽 = 𝄾). Four sixteenth rests equal a quarter rest (𝄽𝄽𝄽𝄽 = 𝄽).
- When consecutive sixteenth notes are written they are joined together (♬♬♬♬) by double beams.
- Sixteenth notes are counted as "one e and a two e and a" (♬♬♬♬ ♬♬♬♬). Pay special attention to the order of the strokes.
  1 e + a 2 e + a

Note that when there are two consecutive F's (♩ ♬ | ♬♬♬♬ | ♬♬♬♬), the fader should be closed when you pull backward. Closing the fader will shut off the sound when you pull back. This allows you to reset and be in position for the next forward stroke.

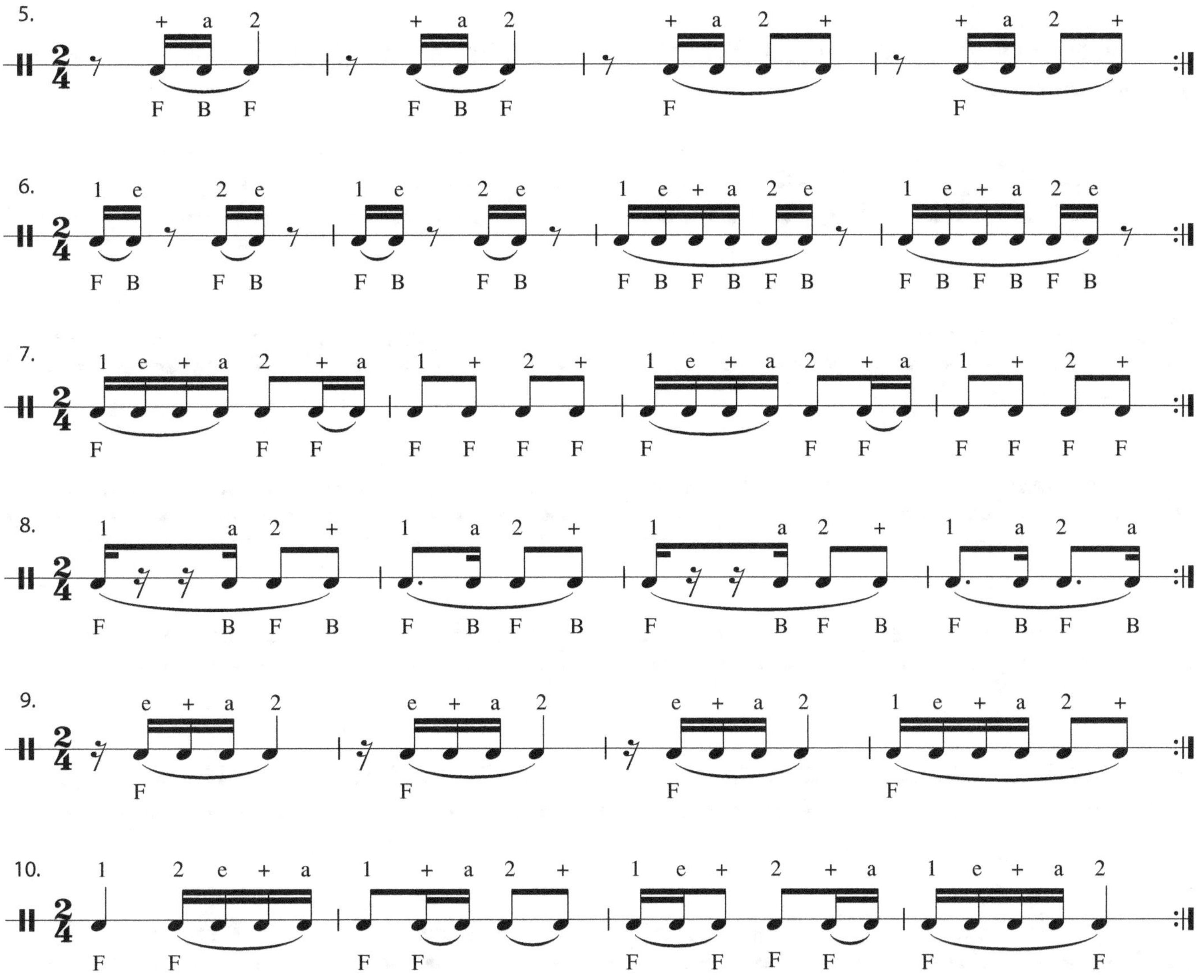
5.
+ a 2 | + a 2 | + a 2 + | + a 2 +
F B F | F B F | F | F
6.
1 e 2 e | 1 e 2 e | 1 e + a 2 e | 1 e + a 2 e
F B F B | F B F B | F B F B F B | F B F B F B
7.
1 e + a 2 + a | 1 + 2 + | 1 e + a 2 + a | 1 + 2 +
F F F | F F F F | F F F | F F F F
8.
1 a 2 + | 1 a 2 + | 1 a 2 + | 1 a 2 a
F B F B | F B F B | F B F B | F B F B
9.
e + a 2 | e + a 2 | e + a 2 | 1 e + a 2 +
F | F | F | F
10.
1 2 e + a | 1 + a 2 + | 1 e + 2 + a | 1 e + a 2
F F | F F | F F F F | F F

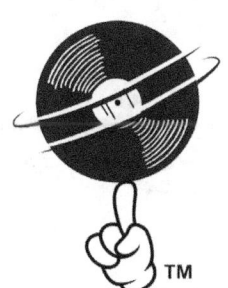

Lesson 19

This lesson consists of sixteenth-note rhythms in 4/4 time. Pay attention to the strokes and keep a steady tempo.

Lesson 20

This is a continuation of the previous lesson with more rhythmic variations.

Lesson 21

Here's a consolidation of the previously studied material. Observe the strokes and keep a steady tempo.

Lesson 22 – Playing Exercise 6

Now try these two Playing Exercises in 4/4 time, which also continue the study of sixteenth-note rhythms.

THE "DROP"

Lesson 23

An "open fader" is one where the fader is left open so the turntable sound comes through. This lesson introduces the open fader technique that is commonly referred to as the "drop."

- Begin by releasing the record at the start of the sound.
- Use your hand to stop the record before the sound ends and pull the record back to the start of the sound.
- The dotted slur (⌣) and (♩) are used to notate this technique.
    - When the dotted slur is noted, the fader remains in the open position.

Note that this lesson incorporates three techniques: the "drop," the "the chirp," and the "baby scratch."

Lesson 24

This is a continuation of the previously studied exercise that introduced 16th notes. Count out loud and maintain an even tempo.

Lesson 25

"THE CUT"

Here is the technique that is often referred to as the "cut."

- Begin this exercise by releasing the record at the start of the sound.
- Use your hand to stop the record before the sound ends.
- Move the cross fader to the closed position and pull the record back to the start of the sound.
- Closing the fader will shut off the sound of the backward stroke.
- Again, the dotted slur (⌣⋯) notates the release of the record.
- Use the rests as an opportunity to reset and return to the start of the sound.
    o The rests will allow you to be in position for the next time you release the record.

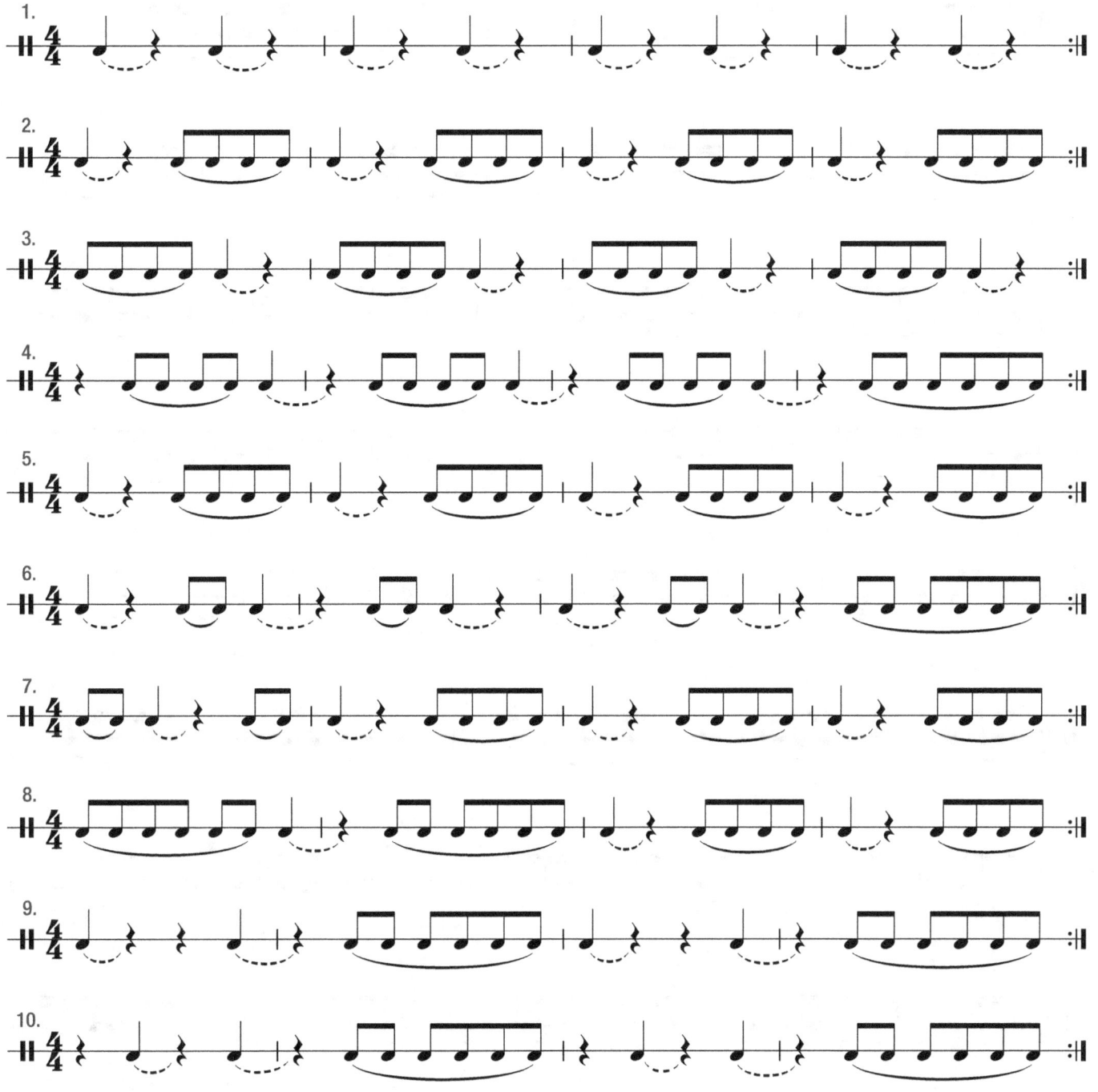

51

Lesson 26

This lesson continues the study of the previous exercise with the addition of 16th notes.

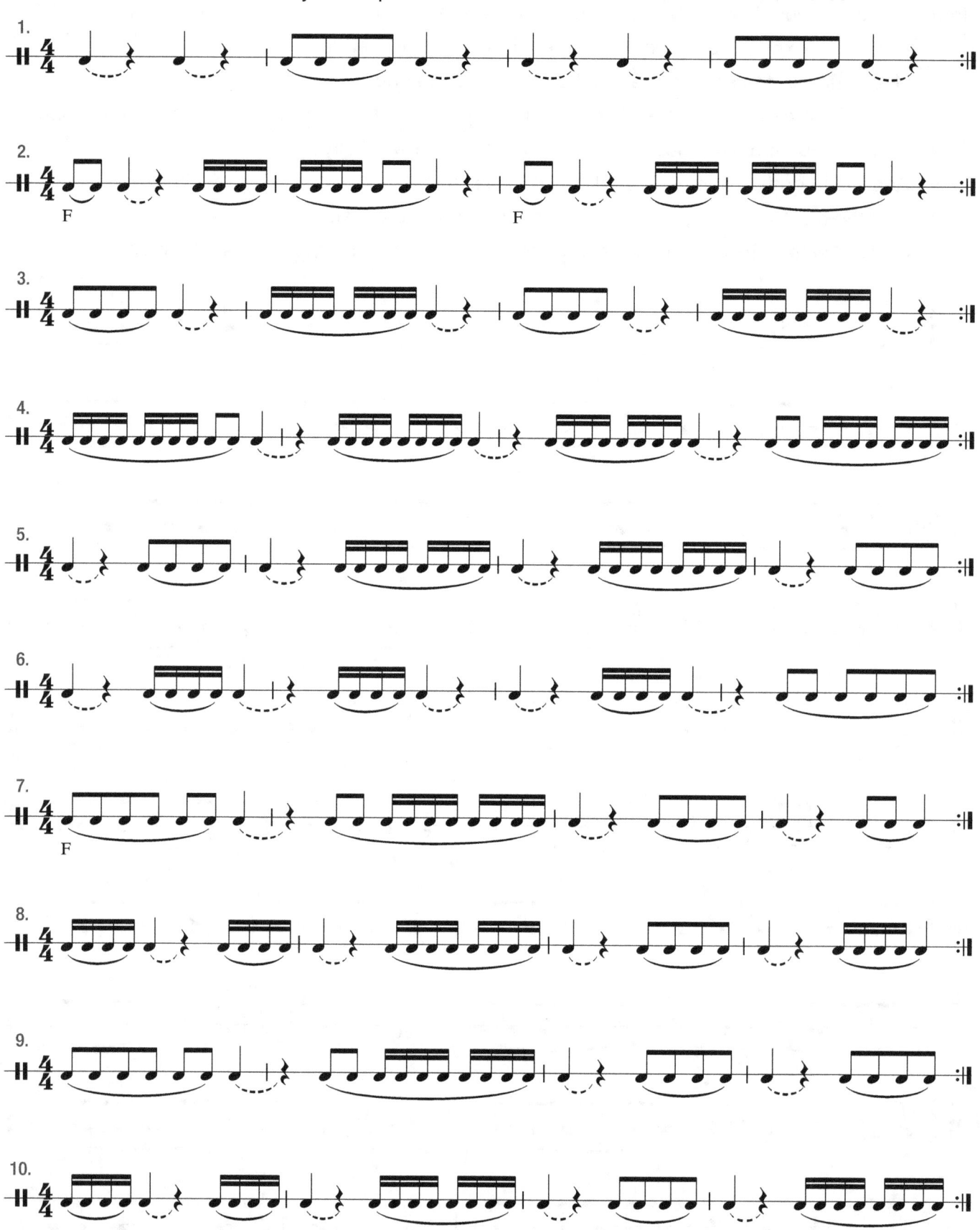

Lesson 27

Now, here is a combination of the "drop," "chirp," "cut," and "baby scratch" techniques. Count out loud and maintain a steady tempo.

Lesson 28

This lesson continues the previous exercise with the addition of the sixteenth note rest.

Lesson 29 — Playing Exercise 7

These Playing Exercises add to the skills of the previously covered material.

Lesson 30

This lesson adds "rhythmic variation." Incorporate these rhythms into your improvisation. Practice the lesson slowly at first.

Lesson 31

Here's a continuation of the previous exercise with a focus on sixteenth and eighth rests.

Lesson 32 – Playing Exercise 8

These Playing Exercises continue the study of the previously covered material. Play slowly at first and maintain an even tempo.

DYNAMICS DRILLS

Dynamics Drill 1

Here's a Dynamics Drill for practice…Apply this exercise to the "Baby Scratch" and "Chirp."

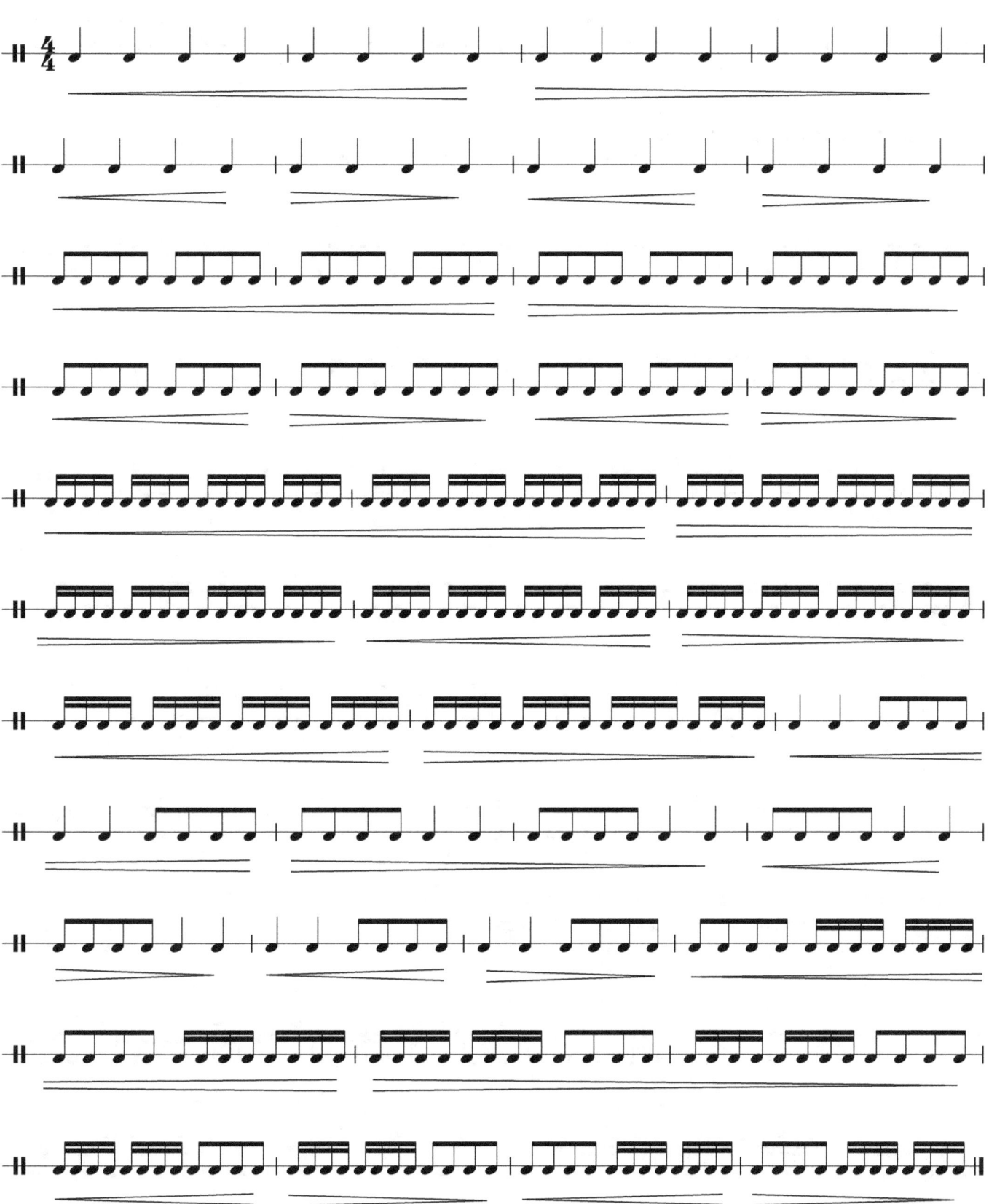

Dynamics Drill 2

Another Dynamics Drill for practice, but this one stressing accents. Apply this exercise to the "Baby Scratch" and "Chirp."

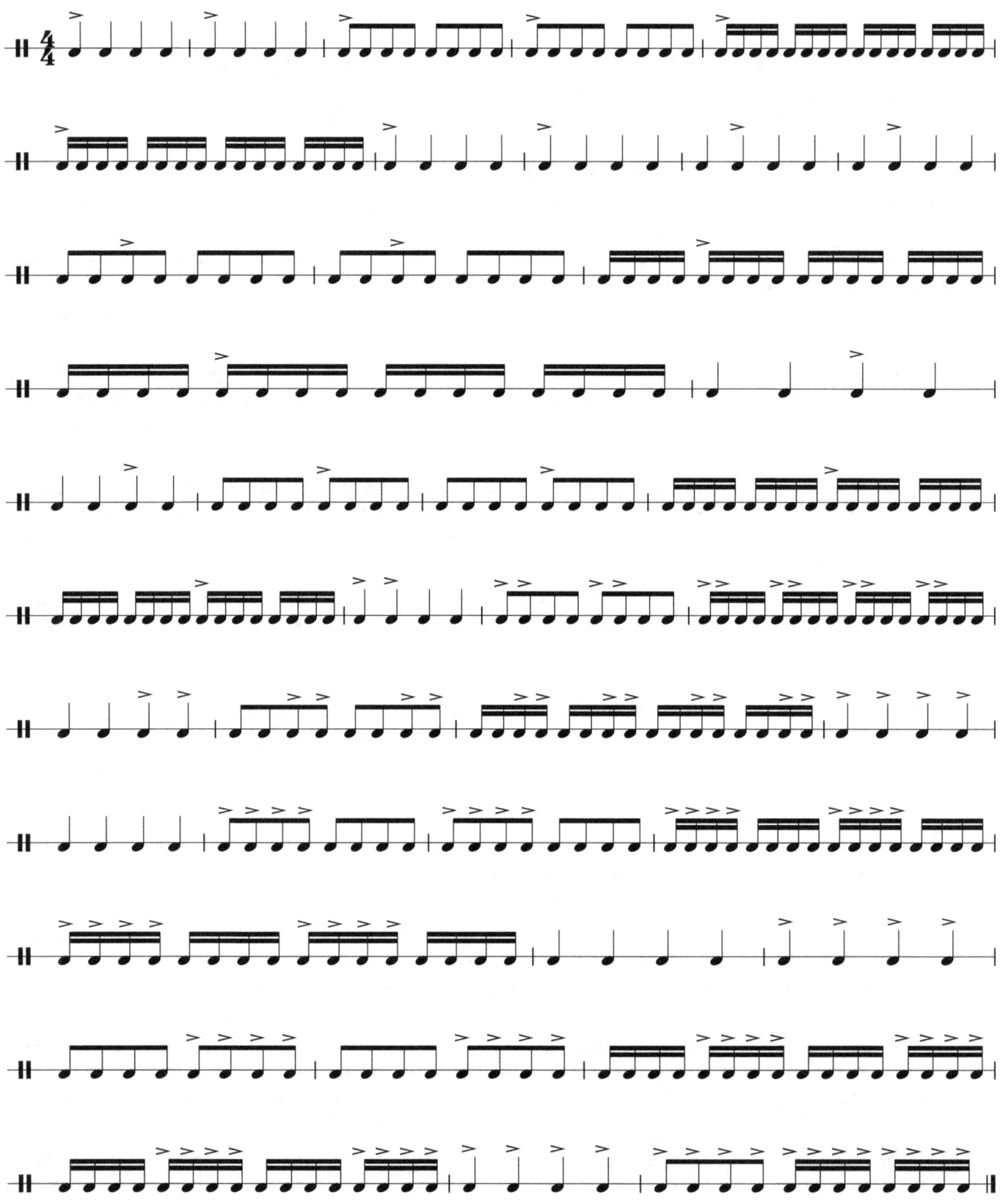

Dynamics Drill 3

This Drill combines dynamics with accents for practice. Apply this exercise to the "Baby Scratch" and "Chirp."

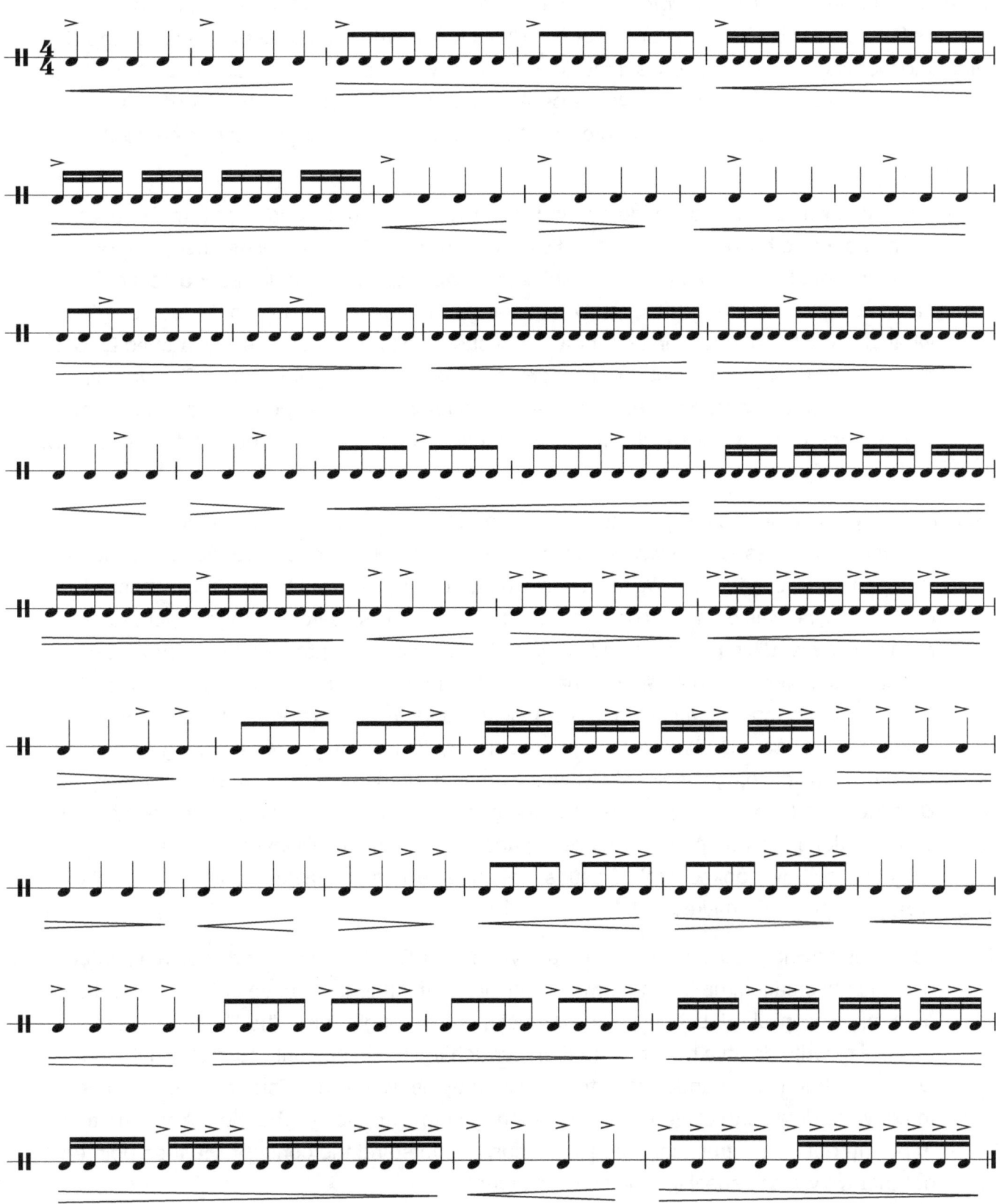

ABOUT THE AUTHORS

How We Got Here

Scratching Made Easy Turntable Method—Book 1: A Guide to Scratching was written by brothers Dwayne / DJ Ronin (Tokyo) and Jason Bullock. Dwayne is an underground Hip Hop DJ living and working in Tokyo. Jason is a music enthusiast with a percussion background, working in corporate America. The story of how this book came together, despite the brothers living on opposite sides of the world, is one of determination, cooperation, dialogue, and even a little fate…

Dwayne: There was some knowledge missing from my DJing, but I couldn't put my finger on it. I managed to build up a pretty good skill set through pride and persistence, but for some reason, I always felt uncomfortable. Over the years in the underground scene, I came across a lot of good Scratch DJs. I wondered "How is this guy right here doing what is in my head, but I can't do it myself? I should be able to do this." I watched DVDs, then tutorial after tutorial, but never progressed the way I thought I should. The first time I reached out to my younger brother, Jason, was because I was spending too much time putting together sets. I instinctively knew what songs went together, but I didn't know why, so I asked Jason.

Jason: During this time, we talked almost every night, but for some reason, we hadn't specifically discussed our own musical worlds. Our conversations were mostly about life in Japan and life in the US. We stayed in touch, but we never talked about our musical goals. Dwayne was on a mission to be a better DJ; he was searching for answers to his problems by watching tutorials and scratch DVDs. I was trying to be a better producer. But we really weren't too aware of what each other was doing. I'd been a percussionist since the fourth grade, which led to my making beats as I got older. Taking classes in college, I'd always been interested in music theory. While Dwayne was making a name for himself in Tokyo, I, coincidentally, was watching tutorials on elementary jazz theory. Dwayne asked me why two songs sounded good together, and this led to some excellent conversations (over a period of five years) about music theory. Dwayne was making progress, so I overlooked a lot of issues, because he was just making common mistakes that the average DJ makes.

Dwayne: I was having problems scratching a rhythm, so I called Jason for advice. In a heated, pivotal conversation, he told me I was struggling with timing, because I didn't understand rhythm. I was insulted, because I knew music, and I thought that I "had" rhythm. Jason told me to write down a rhythm, and then scratch it. I said I can only scratch what I feel. On top of that, I didn't understand the terminology he was using. This was the first time that I wrote down and played rhythms. I managed to write down what he asked, and tried to play it, but I was struggling, because I didn't understand the concept. He then pointed out that we weren't speaking the same "language."

Jason: I gave Dwayne some basic rhythms to prove a point, knowing he was going to make mistakes. I wanted him to see that he didn't understand the fundamentals. After making several failed attempts, he asked what he could do to fix this problem, so I sent him some elementary exercises. He asked "How good could I be if I did this?" I told him that with practice, he could be as good as he wanted to be. I explained that theory is the equalizer. Some people are naturally talented, and scratching comes easy for them. But with theory, you can write out with music notation the complex rhythms that the best DJs are doing, develop a learning process that allows you to do the same, and then eventually put your own twist on it. With practice and dedication, I told him, theoretically he could be one of the best in the world!

Dwayne: After 10 minutes of attempting the sheet music that Jason sent me, I realized that my timing was terrible, and that I had a hard time controlling the record and staying on beat. I also knew exactly what Jason had given me. It was the answer to my dreams—the tools for building a foundation. It took out all of the guesswork, and the mystery was gone. I could see the learning progression on the page, and I could feel myself getting better with each line. After practicing, I called Jason and said "We have to write a book." A lot of pieces had to fall into place. Without realizing it, we were working on different things that eventually came to be this collaboration. Opportunities to move forward, through obstacles such as time zone differences—Baltimore and Tokyo—miraculously fell into place. My brother and I were on different paths, that eventually came together.

Jason: When we began, the notation system we needed didn't exist. I had to create it, but before I could get started, I had to learn about scratching. I had to learn the names of the different scratch techniques and how they were executed. I grew up around DJs, had been on turntables, and was familiar with the sounds of the scratches. But until then, when it came to scratching, I had never put much thought into what the DJs were actually doing. I began by analyzing tutorials and scratch routines. I studied the rhythms and visualized what the different techniques would look like on paper. Once I became familiar with the techniques, I identified which ones were appropriate for an elementary book. I wrote out 24 lessons, and Dwayne had to learn the notation system. I knew that once he learned the system, he would be able to provide the feedback needed to complete the book. The funny thing is that when I said to Dwayne that we had to speak the same language, I wasn't expecting that I had to learn his! Over the course of eight years (thirteen years after our first conversation), everything came full circle. The book evolved naturally, and it changed the trajectory of our lives.

Dwayne: Over time, I came to understand that learning music is a process—it's not overnight. Through music, I learned the true meaning of "what you reap is what you sow." For me to become proficient and musically trained took years, but I know now that if you have a process and a method, it can be done. I'm living proof. Our book is the result, and a roadmap for other DJs wanting to take their scratching to the next level. We hope that this transforms your lives, as it did ours.

Enjoy

www.ingramcontent.com/pod-product-compliance
Lightning Source LLC
Chambersburg PA
CBHW081627100526
44590CB00021B/3641